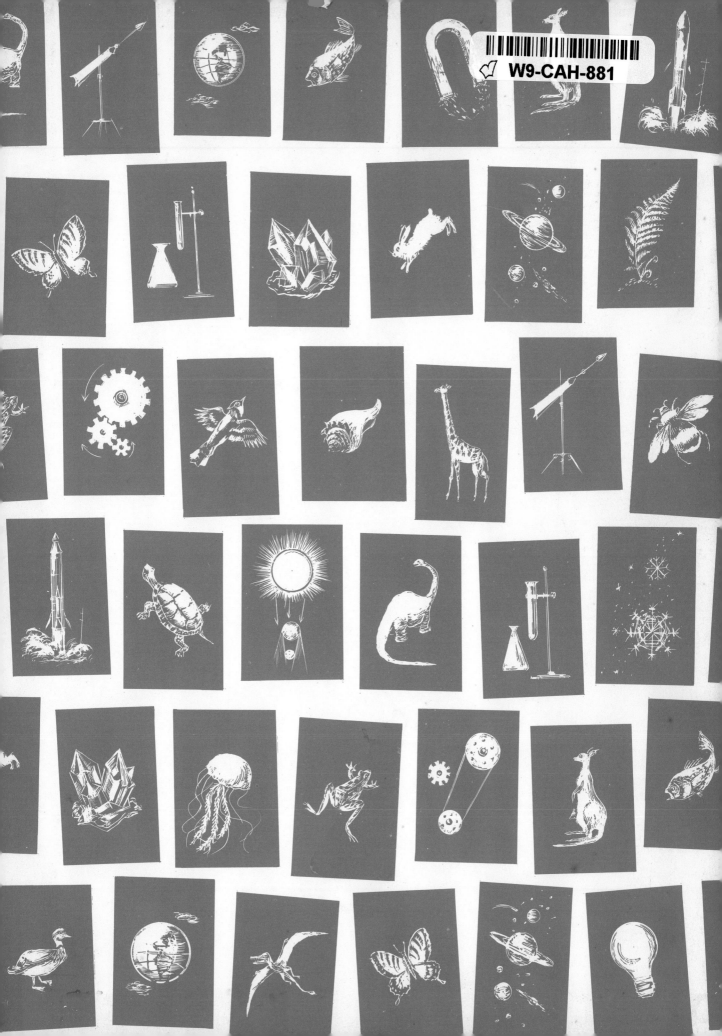

THE HOW AND WHY WONDER BOOK OF

BEGINNING
SCIENCE

By DR. JEROME J. NOTKIN, Science Supervisor,
Suffolk County, N. Y.
Professor, Hofstra College
and SIDNEY GULKIN, M. S. in Ed.,
Teacher, New York City

Illustrated by WILLIAM FRACCIO
and TONY TALLARICO

Editorial Production: DONALD D. WOLF

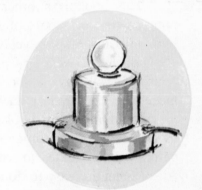

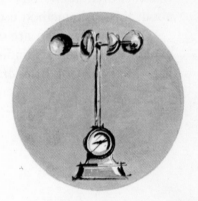

Edited under the supervision of
   Dr. Paul E. Blackwood
   Washington, D. C.

Text and illustrations approved by

   Oakes A. White
   Brooklyn Children's Museum
   Brooklyn, New York

GROSSET & DUNLAP • Publishers • NEW YORK

Introduction

This book is another in a series of *How and Why Wonder Books* planned to open doors of scientific knowledge to young readers. A quick look into the book reveals that it deals with several important areas of science: light, weather, plants, machines, and electricity. This general approach will have a special appeal to readers who wish an overview of more than one area of science within a single book.

In addition, this book helps the reader himself become more scientific by emphasizing experiments as a way of making discoveries. Young investigators will be pleased to see that over two dozen experiments are suggested. All of them are easy to do and require only simple equipment. They can be done at home by parents and children together, or they can be done at school. In either event, children can have fun and, at the same time, learn a great deal about this basic method used by scientists.

Youngsters who are eager to learn will find this book of great help in exploring and understanding their environment, and they will want to add it to their shelf of *How and Why Wonder Books*.

Paul E. Blackwood

Library of Congress Catalog Card Number: 60-51558

Foreword

This is a book about basic ideas in science. You don't have to be a college student or even a high-school boy or girl to understand these ideas. Try to do some of the things suggested here, and you will begin to understand why science is so important in our lives. You will see for yourself how weather instruments work—how they help in predicting the weather. You will take a nail, some insulated wire, and a dry cell, and make it behave like a magnet whenever you want to, and then take its power away. Just like that.

No, this is not a book to teach you magic or tricks. It's even better. It's a book about old ideas that will remain new and always true. These ideas will help you make things now to have fun with, and later on will help you build bridges, invent new machines, and perhaps discover new ways to promote long life and good health.

Do as many of the projects as you can. If you don't succeed the first or second time, try again. You will have lots of fun trying.

Good luck!

Jerome J. Notkin
Sidney Gulkin

CONTENTS

Light in Our Lives

Important Words

Photon: A tiny bundle of light energy.

Reflection: Bouncing of light rays in straight lines.

Refraction: Bending of light rays as they go from one substance to another.

The tremendous gains made in the area of artificial lighting can be measured by the contrast shown above.

Have you ever heard someone say, "Turn the light on — I can't see a thing"? Or: "We'll have to wait until the sun rises before we can see"?

Without light we would be lost. A long time ago people depended upon the light of the sun to do their work. They would begin to work when the sun rose and would stop when the sun set.

Then people discovered fire and found that it could light rooms at night. You know the famous story about how Abe Lincoln used to read a great deal in front of his fireplace just to get the light from the fire. Of course, many people used candles, if they could afford them. Later a fuel—kerosene— was used in special lamps.

Still later, gas—illuminating gas— gave us light in our homes and even on our streets.

Finally electricity came along, so that we now have all the artificial light we need.

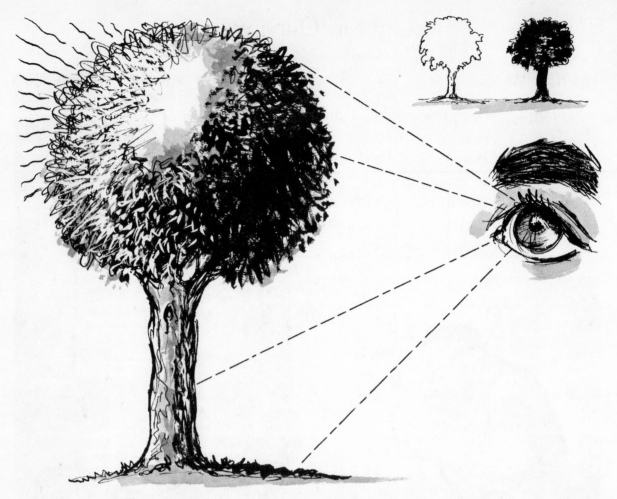

Light is wonderful. But what is it? Let's see. Some of the greatest minds in the history of mankind have been asking and trying to answer the question: "What is light?"

Among the people who helped make great discoveries about light were such scientific giants as Sir Isaac Newton, James Clerk-Maxwell, and Max Planck. It is Planck's theory that tells us that light is a flow of bundles of energy. These bundles of energy are referred to as PHOTONS. This is, of course, a very simple attempt to explain a difficult theory. As we learn more science, we will learn a great deal more about light.

Scientists are funny people in a way. Once they find out one thing, they begin

When photons hit an object which absorbs them, the object looks dark. If the photons bounce back to your eye, the object reflects light. See diagram above.

wondering how to find out more. That is what happened to the great Danish scientist, Olaus Roemer. He figured that the speed of light was about 186,000 miles per second. He was fairly accurate. Mind you, this was in 1675. In our own times an American scientist, Albert Michelson, in a very difficult experiment found that light travels at 186,285 miles per second. As you can see, our friend Roemer came close to the accurate measurements Dr. Michelson made.

You can find out many interesting things about light and have fun at the same time.

How Can You Read Mirror Writing?

You will use:

Three mirrors about 4 by 4 inches
One shoebox without a cover
Cellophane tape
Front page of a newspaper
Scissors

Do this:

Stand one mirror up in a corner of the shoebox. Place a second mirror alongside it, so that both mirrors touch in one corner of the box at right angles to each other.

Tape the mirrors in place.

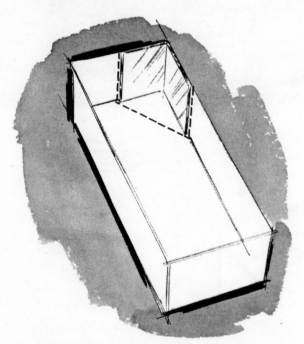

Preparing a box with mirrors to read mirror-writing

Cut out the corner of the box with the mirrors, cutting across the dotted line along the bottom of the box.

Now mount three or four words of a newspaper headline on a piece of cardboard. Our headline reads: "CITY IN DARKNESS."

Now place the headline in front of your corner mirrors. Look right into the corner between the mirrors. Is the writing reversed, or can you read it?

It should read: "CITY IN DARKNESS."

Place it in front of the third mirror. Can you read it, or is it reversed?

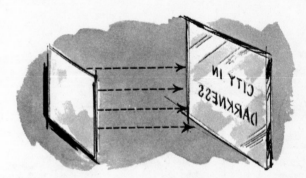

The third mirror reverses the writing.

Why does it work?

What actually happened is that one of the corner mirrors reversed the writing, while the second mirror re-reversed it back to the normal order of writing we can read.

This is not a trick. It is a science experiment that any boy or girl can do. You will accomplish two things—learn an idea in science and have a lot of fun.

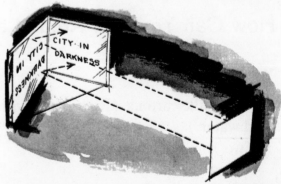

The second mirror re-reverses writing, now readable.

How Can You See Around a Corner?

You will use:

Two milk cartons (Rinse well with cold water.)

Two small mirrors

Adhesive tape

Knife

Do this:

Cut off the tops of both milk cartons.

Insert the open end of one carton into the open end of the other, so that they form a 16-inch tube.

One inch from the bottom of one of

the cartons, cut out a window in the side 1½ inches high.

Cut a slit in the same side, ½ inch from the bottom.

Insert a mirror, face up, in the slit until one end rests along the back of the carton. Secure the mirror with tape at the angle shown in the illustration.

Do the same thing with the opposite side of the other carton.

The reflecting sides of the mirrors should be facing each other.

You have made a periscope.

Try looking out the window by looking into the lower part of the periscope, while the upper part is above the window ledge. You can look out the window or around corners while you are out of sight.

The periscope which you can build yourself is based on the same principle as a real one found in a sub.

Why does it work?

The reason you can do all of these things is that light travels in a straight line. The mirrors reflect the rays of light.

Try reading through a periscope. Let someone hold a newspaper and see if you can read the headlines. Is it mirror writing? Can you explain it?

The reason you were able to read the headline in the periscope is because mirror A made mirror-writing which mirror B reversed to normal writing.

9

How Can You Bend Light?

You will use:

A large, clear drinking glass
Teaspoon

Do this:

Fill the glass with water.
Place a spoon in the glass.
Look at the spoon from many different positions. The spoon will appear to be broken.

Why does it work?

Light travels faster through air than it does through water. In passing in or out of water, light rays change their direction slightly.

This is called refraction. It occurs when light passes from air to a denser material such as water or glass, where its speed is slowed down.

The word "refraction" is often confused with "reflection."

That often happens, because many science words for different things sound alike. You can play a game—a science word game—with your friends. See if they can tell you the difference between sound-alike words.

The oar in the water (or a teaspoon in a glass) appears broken. It only seems so due to refraction of light.

The light "bounces" from the mirror to the ceiling.

How Can You Bounce Light?

You will use:

A small mirror

A flashlight

Do this:

Hold the mirror so that you catch some light right on it, and direct it to a wall or ceiling.

Move the mirror quickly. Move it slowly. Direct it to other parts of the room.

Why does it work?

Some rays of light landed on the mirror and bounced right off—that is, the light rays were reflected to the wall.

If you notice carefully, you will see that the rays reflect off the mirror at exactly the same slant, or angle, that they hit it. This shows us that light travels in straight lines.

We know from experience and scientific observation that white materials reflect the sun's rays, while darker or black materials absorb them. That is

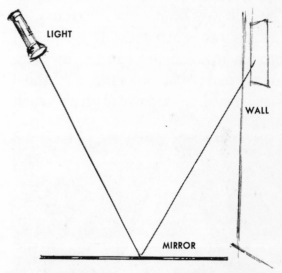

Rays reflect off mirror at the same angle they hit it.

why people living in warm climates wear white clothing. Do you remember pictures you have seen of Arabs in the desert? It is always cooler to wear a white shirt or dress in the summertime so that the sun's rays bounce off and away from you.

Can You See a Rainbow Other Than in the Sky?

You will use:

A prism or a triangular ornamental crystal from a chandelier

Do this:

Hold the prism in a path of sunlight so that light will pass somewhere through the center.

Don't be discouraged if a rainbow is not seen at once. Move the prism until you begin to see beautiful colors.

Why does it work?

When light travels from a lighter substance such as air to a heavier substance such as glass or water, it slows down. The light rays bend, or are refracted.

Therefore, when white light is passed through a prism, we can see its component parts—the colors of a rainbow —as they are separated from each other.

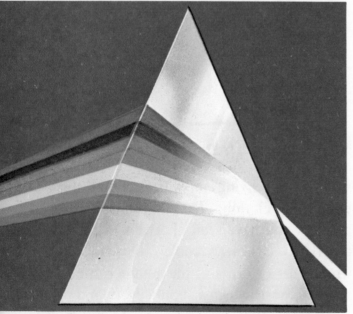

The prism breaks up bright light into its components.

How Can You Burn Paper Without a Match?

You will use:

Magnifying glass
Piece of paper
Metal pan
Water

Do this:

Place the paper in a metal pan as a safety precaution.

Try to catch some rays of the sun on your glass, and direct them onto the piece of paper.

Hold the glass long enough and the

How Can You Make a Rainbow Without a Prism?

You will use:

Pan with water
Mirror

Do this:

Place a mirror at an angle inside the water-filled pan.

Place the pan in the path of a strong source of light. The rays should strike the mirror in the water.

A rainbow should be on the wall.

Why does it work?

As light struck the mirror, it was reflected. However, it was also refracted, or bent, because the rays passed through more than one substance.

The bending light rays separated into their many parts, each one traveling at a different frequency. The result was the rainbow colors on the wall.

paper will begin to smoke and catch fire.

Pour water into the pan. Be sure that the fire is completely out.

Why does it work?

When the rays of the sun struck the convex lens (that's the type of lens a magnifying glass is), they converged, or were refracted to one point. Remember that the sun gives light and heat. The heat was so concentrated that it ignited the paper.

Fire is not a toy to play with. A good scientist is a careful one. Be sure to do experiments involving fire in the presence of an adult.

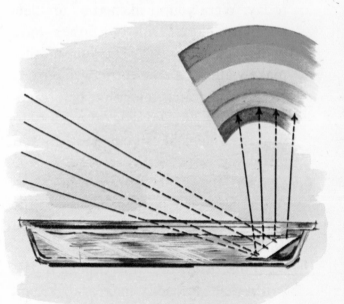

Electricity—Magic at Your Finger Tips

Important Words

Dry Cell: A zinc container filled with a chemical paste and a carbon rod to produce electricity.

Electron: Tiny particle that carries a minus charge of electricity.

Fuse: Acts as a policeman to warn us of danger. The fuse melts when too many electrons are flowing. This breaks the circuit.

Volt: Unit for measuring electrical pressure.

Watt: Unit for measuring electrical power.

We have been told that magic has no place in science. But if Michael Faraday could see some of the modern uses for electricity, he might say, "It *must* be magic!"

Just think how you used electricity today. Were you awakened by an electric alarm clock? Did your father shave with an electric razor? Did your mother make waffles on an electric waffle iron?

Did you watch television before going to school? Did you ever stop to wonder what makes your doorbell and telephone work?

Were the lights on in your classroom? Did your principal speak to the school over the loudspeaker? Did you see a movie or a filmstrip in class?

Think of all the other things in the world that electricity makes work, and you will see why anyone might use the word "magic" for it.

A magic trick, however, cannot usually be repeated successfully at home. But many scientific experiments can be carried out by anyone. In fact, it isn't always necessary to have a great deal of equipment. Much of it can be homemade.

So let's forget the word "magic" and replace it with "understanding" and "knowledge."

When a scientist is puzzled by something, he tries to find the answer by doing several things. He observes whatever puzzles him very carefully. He then writes down what he sees. Then he studies this information to see if he can get an idea about it. He calls this idea a theory. Next, he goes about trying to prove whether or not the theory is correct.

Scientists have a theory about the

nature of electricity. To understand this theory, we must begin with another theory. This one deals with the "building blocks" of the universe.

Everything you can think of is made up of molecules, the smallest particle into which anything can be divided and still keep its original qualities. If we break down a molecule, we have atoms different from our molecule. For instance, water (a liquid) is made up of two atoms of hydrogen and one of oxygen (both gases until they combine to form water). If we break down the water molecule, the hydrogen and oxygen return to their original state as gases.

All things in the world are made up of combinations of about 100 atoms. That is why we call atoms the "building blocks" of the universe.

Atoms, themselves, are composed of

In the year 1752, Benjamin Franklin, the famous American statesman and scientist, proved that lightning was a form of electricity. He attached a metal key to the cord of a kite and one day, during a thunderstorm, Franklin flew his kite. Whenever lightning hit the flying kite above, sparks flew from the key.

still smaller particles called electrons, protons, neutrons, and several others.

Scientists tell us that electricity is made up of the electrons that are part of all material. When we get these electrons to move, we have an electric current—electricity.

We make these electrons move—so

Hydroelectric plant: The great force of the falling water collected behind the dam activates the generator.

that they can work for us—in generators which may be far from our homes or factories.

Fuel such as coal or oil is used to make these generators turn and make the electrons flow. Often steam is used. Sometimes falling water from a dam turns fan-shaped wheels called turbines. A shaft is attached to each turbine. When that shaft turns inside a generator, or dynamo, electricity comes out.

The electricity—or moving electrons—is pushed through wires toward our homes, factories, farms, and wherever it is needed.

This push, or pressure, is measured in volts. The voltage in the wires along the way is very high, but when it comes into your house, it has been reduced to 110 to 220 volts.

Now it can be used to operate your television set, electric trains, toaster, vacuum cleaner, and many other appliances.

How did people light their homes and streets before Thomas Edison invented the electric light?

The cave men used torches.
The ancient Greeks and Romans had oil lamps to light their way.

The early settlers in this country used candles.

Later, a way was found to use gas for light and kerosene lamps.

But it wasn't until about eighty years ago that the first electric light was used. A light bulb is called an incandescent lamp. This means that the wire in the bulb is heated until it glows. Our sun is also incandescent.

17

Perhaps you are lucky enough to be in a new school. It is likely that your room is lighted by another type of lamp —a fluorescent lamp.

Fluorescent lamp.

People often ask, "What is the real difference between the incandescent lamp and the fluorescent lamp?"

The main difference is in the way they give off light. The incandescent filament, made of tungsten, is heated by the electricity flowing through it to such an extent that it glows white hot.

In the fluorescent lamp, moving electrons pass through the vapor that fills the tube. This produces ultraviolet rays which strike chemicals that coat the inside of the tube. The chemicals glow, and we have light.

We get more light and less heat with fluorescent lamps.

How Does an Incandescent Lamp Glow?

You will use:

Dry cell
Short piece of iron wire
Pliers

Do this:

Connect a short piece of iron wire to the two terminals of a dry cell. In seconds the wire will become hot and will glow.

Note: This reduces the life of the dry cell, so do not keep the wire connected for too long.

Caution: Disconnect the wire with a pair of pliers to avoid burning yourself.

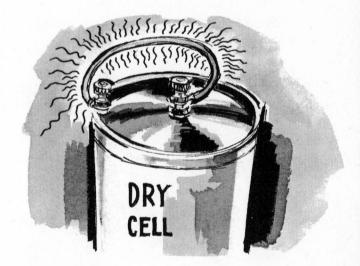

Why it works:

The wire completes the circuit so that electrons can flow from one terminal of the dry cell to the other.

The electricity is changed into heat and light energy.

This is similar to the way an incandescent lamp works.

How Can a Switch Help Us?

You will use:

Dry cell (large)
Light bulb
Socket
Insulated copper wire
Piece of metal
Block of wood
Two nails
Hammer

Do this:

Take a piece of metal—4 inches long, 1 inch wide (you can cut it from a tin can if you are careful).

Nail one end of it on the block of wood.

Place another nail in the wood under the other end of the metal.

Do not place either nail all the way down in the wood.

Be sure that the loose end of the metal is not resting on the nail beneath it.

Now you have a switch.

With wires all in place, the circuit has been closed.

Connect one wire from either terminal of the dry cell to the nail under the metal.

Be sure to strip the insulation from the ends of all the wires you use.

Connect a second wire from the other terminal of the dry cell to either terminal of the miniature socket.

Connect a third wire from the other terminal of the socket to the nail holding the strip of metal in place.

Now press the switch.

If you have made all the connections right, the circuit now is closed, and the light will go on.

Save this switch. You will probably use it many times.

Why it works:

If you have a large dry cell, notice the two terminals at the top.

This makes connecting wires to it much easier than connecting them to a small flashlight cell.

But all of these projects can be done with either cell, except that the large cell lasts longer and is easier to work with.

Each cell gives 1½ volts.

The switch is a convenient way to open and close a circuit. It is easier than connecting and disconnecting wires. It is also a safe way to turn lights and other electrical appliances on and off.

How Can You Make an Electromagnet?

You will use:

Dry cell
Wire
Switch
Large nail
Small nails or paper clips

Do this:

Wind about ten turns of wire around a large nail.

Strip the insulation from the ends of the wire.

Connect one end of the wire to one terminal of a dry cell, and the other end to a terminal of the switch.

Prepare a second wire. Connect this wire to the other terminal of the dry cell and the other end of the switch.

Now close the switch, and try to pick up paper clips or small nails with the large nail. Open the switch, and the small nails or paper clips will fall.

Why it works:

The electricity from one part of the dry cell flows through the many turns of wire back into the dry cell.

When electricity flows through a wire, the wire has magnetic power around it. If the wire happens to be in the form of a coil, the magnetism is even stronger.

An iron nail inside the coil becomes a magnet. This is true only so long as the electricity is flowing in the circuit. It is a magnet when you want it to be.

DRY CELL

ELECTROMAGNET

How Can You Make a Horseshoe Electromagnet?

You will use:

Long, thin bolt (or U-bolt)
Insulated copper wire
Dry cell
Switch
Small nails or paper clips

Do this:

Wind several layers of wire around one arm, then the other, of a U-bolt. (Such a bolt, if unobtainable, may be made by bending a long thin bolt into a U-shape, using a vise.)

Strip the insulation from the ends of the wire.

Connect one end of a piece of wire to one terminal of the dry cell, and the other end to the terminal of the switch.

Connect a second piece of wire between the dry cell and the switch.

Close the switch. How many paper clips or nails can you pick up with your horseshoe electromagnet?

Open the switch. What happens? Try this several times.

Why it works:

We already know why an electromagnet works. (See previous experiment.)

What are the advantages of an electromagnet shaped like this?

We are now able to take advantage of the magnetism produced in both ends, or poles, of the electromagnet. When both poles are near each other, we get up to twice the strength that a straight bolt gives — if the number of turns of wire is the same on each side.

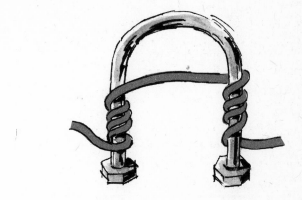

How to wind a bolt

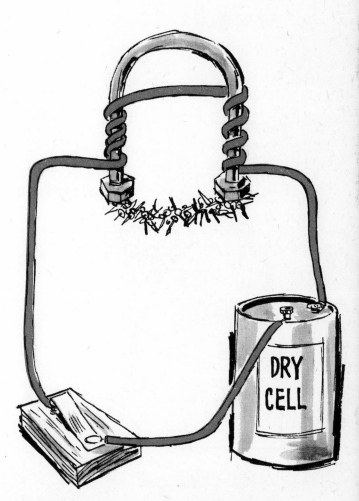

Horseshoe electromagnet will produce magnetism.

How Can You Test the Polarity of an Electromagnet?

You will use:

Electromagnets you have made
Switch
Insulated copper wire
Dry cell
Magnetic compass

Do this:

Connect your horseshoe magnet to a dry cell and a switch, as suggested in the previous experiment.

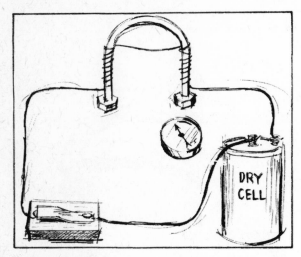

Place a compass as shown and close the switch.

Wires connected to the dry cell are now reversed.

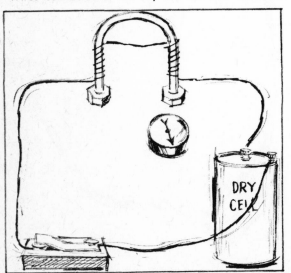

Bring a magnetic compass near one of the poles of your electromagnet. Close the switch. What happens to the needle of the compass? Which pole of the compass was attracted to the pole of your electromagnet?

Move the compass near the other pole of the electromagnet. Close the switch again. What happens this time?

Why it works:

We know that the opposite poles of a magnet—that is, north and south—attract each other. Like poles—north and north, or south and south—repel each other. You can tell which pole is which by testing with a magnetic compass. Try to determine the polarity of your horseshoe electromagnet. Remember that the compass itself is a magnet.

What do you think would happen if you reversed the two wires connected to the dry cell? Try it and see how much fun you can have.

Do you see how magnetism and electricity are related?

Our magnet really depends on the electricity it gets from the dry cell.

We find electromagnets all around us. We find them in refrigerators, in television sets, in telephones, in Dad's electric shaver, and in Mother's vacuum cleaner.

Electricity can be your friend or your enemy. Don't try to argue with it. If you make a mistake, it will be too late to say, "I'm sorry." You can use electricity as a powerful and dependable servant if you learn some very important safety rules.

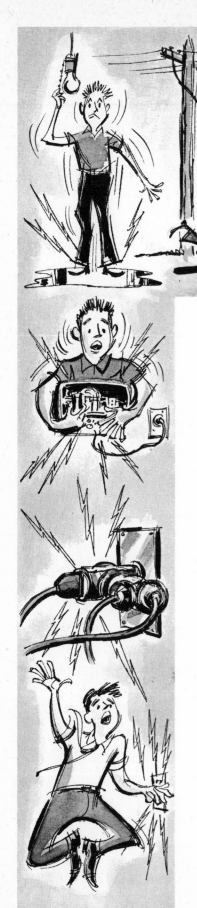

Safety Rules

Never touch a switch with wet or damp hands.

Never overload your connections.

Never poke around a radio or television set if the switch is on.

Never pull the chain of a light bulb if you are standing on a wet floor.

Never, never touch a broken cable after or during a storm, or even if the sun is shining. Call a policeman or a fireman.

Never touch an electrical appliance, switch, radio, or television set while bathing or when wet.

Never put electrical wires under carpets.

Never put a penny in the fuse box. Use a fuse of the proper size.

Never place anything except an electrical plug into a wall socket.

Never remain in a lake during a thunderstorm.

Never remain under or near a tree during an electrical storm or a thunderstorm. Find other shelter quickly.

Many people are interested in forecasts: sailors, farmers, pilots and even those going on a picnic.

Everybody Talks About the Weather

Important Words

Barometer: An instrument used to measure the pressure of the atmosphere.

Thermometer: An instrument used to measure temperature.

Meteorology: The science dealing with the study of weather.

Humidity: Moderate dampness.

Radiosonde: A radio device carried aloft by a balloon, which relays atmospheric pressure, temperature, and humidity.

What is the first thing you do after you wake up each morning? Do you try to get back under the covers for a few more minutes? Do you start to sing? Or do you do what many other people do —peer outdoors to see what kind of weather it is? This helps you decide what type of clothing to wear.

Many people are vitally interested in the weather.

Bad weather might prevent a fisherman or a farmer from earning his living. Think about it for a moment, and you will realize how important this is. Can you understand why pilots receive weather checks regularly while in the air? A skipper of a ship also needs to know what the weather will be like.

Knowing ahead of time what the weather will be is so important to many businesses that special people are hired to provide this information.

The weatherman, as he is called, is really a specially trained scientist in meteorology.

Meteorology is the science of

weather, and the men who study it are called meteorologists.

Meteorologists work for airlines, public utilities, transportation companies, department stores, and the United States Weather Bureau.

No, they do not use a crystal ball. Instead, weather reports from all over the world are studied to determine what kind of weather is moving toward us. The meteorologist uses many instruments to help him in his work.

These instruments tell him the temperature, air pressure, speed and direction of the wind, the amount of moisture in the air—that is, the humidity—the kind of clouds in the sky, the amount of rainfall, and other important information.

Not only does the meteorologist want to know these facts about the air near him, but he also wants the same information about the upper air.

Data about the air fifteen or more miles above the ground is obtained by sending up a large helium-filled balloon. Attached to the balloon is an instrument called a radiosonde which transmits the data to receivers on the ground. Afterward the radiosonde parachutes back to earth and is recovered.

Here are some instruments used by the weatherman. Some of these end in "meter," a Greek word meaning "measure." You can make some of these for your home or classroom.

THERMOMETER . . . . . measures temperature.
BAROMETER . . . . measures pressure.
ANEMOMETER . . . . . measures speed of wind.
WIND VANE . . . . . indicates direction of wind.
HYGROMETER . . . . measures humidity.
RAIN GAUGE . . . . measures amount of rainfall.

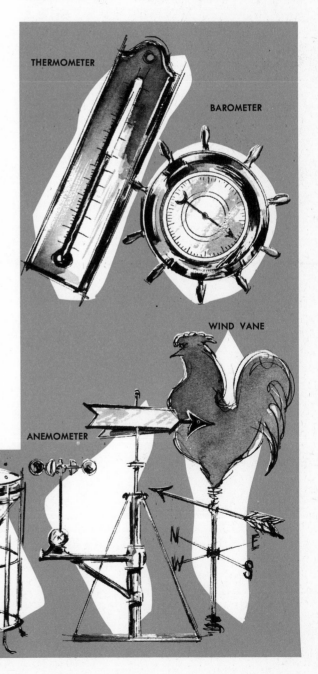

THERMOMETER

BAROMETER

WIND VANE

ANEMOMETER

HYGROMETER

RAIN GAUGE

How Can You Make a Thermometer?

You will use:

Milk bottle with cap
Plastic straw
Wax
Colored water
White card

Do this:

Fill the bottle with colored water.

Place the plastic straw in a hole in the center of the milk-bottle cap.

Melt a little bit of the wax around the straw and around the edge of the cap.

Place a white card behind the straw so that its water level can be easily seen.

Water will expand and rise as air temperature rises.

What will happen?

The water will rise in the straw. As the air temperature increases, the water will expand and rise even higher.

As the temperature decreases, the water will contract, and the level in the straw will come down.

Here is your chance to be really scientific

Place a commercial thermometer next to your homemade one. Draw a line on the white card next to the water level in the straw. On this line write the temperature you read on the commercial thermometer. If you take both thermometers to colder or warmer places and record the commercial thermome-

Compare your thermometer with a commercial one.

ter readings next to the water levels on your homemade scale, you will be able to figure out a scale for your thermometer.

How does a fan blowing on your thermometer affect it? Compare the commercial thermometer with yours.

The cool air from a fan will lower the temperature.

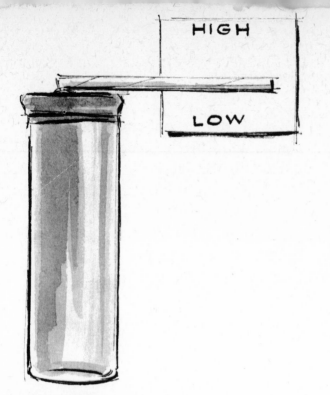

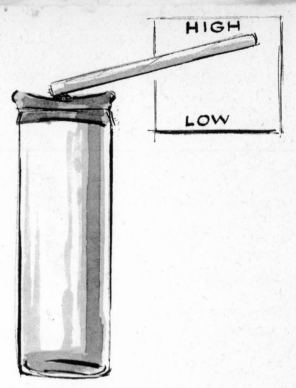

How Can You Test Air Pressure?

You will use:

Olive jar
Rubber balloon
Rubber band
Drinking straw
Glue
White card

Do this:

Cut the balloon so that it can be stretched over the mouth of the jar.

Place the rubber band about the neck of the jar so that the stretched balloon will stay put.

Now place a drop of glue in the center of the piece of balloon.

Place one end of the straw on the glue. Hold it in place until the glue dries.

Place a white card behind the end of the straw.

You have made a barometer.

What will happen?

As the pressure of the air increases, it presses hard in all directions. It presses hard on the jar, on the desk—all over. It also presses on the surface of the balloon, pushing it downward. The end of the straw attached to the balloon dips down, causing the other end to point upward.

This indicates high pressure.

When the air pressure is low, it does not press so hard on objects. If the pressure inside the bottle has more force pushing up than the pressure from the outside pushing downward, the result is that the balloon bulges up, causing the far end of the straw to dip down.

This indicates low pressure.

A rapid drop of pressure usually is an indication that bad weather is coming.

Your next project will be to make a rain gauge. It is another instrument that will help you to know more about the weather.

How Can You Measure Rain in Inches?

You will use:

Olive jar
Ruler

Do this:

Set an olive jar outdoors. After a rainfall, measure the amount of water that has fallen into the jar.

Why does it work?

The amount of rain that collected in your jar during one rainfall can be compared with the amount recorded during another rainfall. For example, if two inches of water are collected one day and one inch the following day, we can say that twice as much rain fell the first day as the second.

We cannot say that three inches of rain fell during those two days. Our gauge is useful as a means of comparing rainfall on different occasions.

How Can You Tell Which Way the Wind Is Blowing?

You will use:

Cardboard
Pair of scissors
Pin
Pencil with eraser

Do this:

Take a piece of cardboard. Cut out an arrow shaped as follows:

Insert a straight pin through the arrow. Push it through the eraser end of an ordinary pencil.

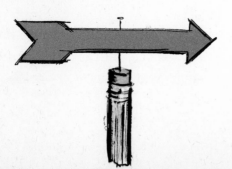

You have made a wind vane.
Take it outdoors. The arrow will turn around in the wind.

What will happen?

The arrow points into the wind. That is, if the arrow points to the north, the wind is coming from the north—it is a north wind.

Set up a real weather bureau, with thermometers, barometers, and a rain gauge to measure the amount of rainfall.

Don't forget the weather maps. The meteorologist uses these maps to find out about weather conditions in other localities, states, and even other countries.

Here are some symbols (used on these weather maps) you should know. They help us learn about the weather, as reported to Washington, D.C., by our country's approximately 300 observing stations. Local stations also send their reports to eight major weather stations located in New York City, Atlanta, Kansas City, Chicago, Los Angeles, Fort Worth, Seattle, and Anchorage, Alaska.

Some of the symbols you should be familiar with are seen below.

The future in weather forecasting is a very bright one.

On April 1, 1960, the United States launched Tiros I, a 270-pound satellite which sent back to earth TV pictures of numerous clouds and storms. The United States Weather Bureau has indicated that meteorological satellite development offers promise of one of the most revolutionary advances in the history of the science of meteorology.

⸠Perhaps some day you will be able to plan a picnic weeks in advance, safe in the knowledge that the weatherman has forecast a sunny day.

Weather bureaus all over the country use certain symbols on their charts to indicate the daily weather picture.

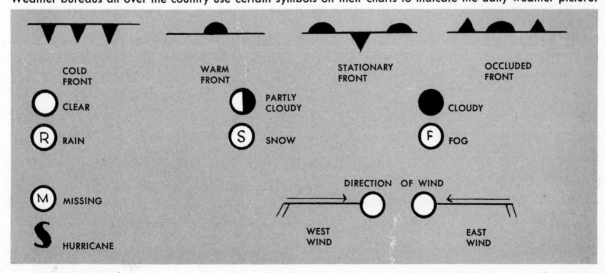

COLD FRONT

WARM FRONT

STATIONARY FRONT

OCCLUDED FRONT

CLEAR

PARTLY CLOUDY

CLOUDY

RAIN

SNOW

FOG

MISSING

HURRICANE

DIRECTION OF WIND

WEST WIND

EAST WIND

Transportation — "Let's Go!"

Important Words

Friction: Resistance to motion caused by the rubbing of one surface against another surface.

Internal Combustion: In an internal combustion engine, such as is found in an automobile, fuel and air mix and explode within the cylinders to cause parts to move.

Jet Propulsion: The force of expanding air or gases rushing out of a rear opening causes an object, such as a rocket or a plane, to move forward.

Steam: Vapor from boiling water. It can be used to make many things move.

In ancient times—and even in some places on earth today—carrying or pushing was man's only means of transporting heavy burdens from one place to another. Later these burdens were placed on animals—oxen, donkeys and horses. In fact, less than a century ago, American Indians carried their goods on travois pulled by horses.

The wheel changed all this. At first, man had a crude, heavy wheel. After many refinements, he developed the wagon wheel and then the automobile wheel, which today moves along highways with speed, safety, and comfort.

How do you think the Egyptians were able to build those huge pyramids without powerful engines to operate cranes?

They used their muscles and their intelligence. We know that the Egyptians had a wheel. It was covered with leather which was secured to the wheel by means of rawhide strips.

Later on, the Greeks and Romans developed better and more decorative wheels for their chariots.

Let's do an experiment to show how rolling helps us move things.

"Let's go" is a common expression meaning to say, "Let's travel," "Let's sail," "Let's fly," or "Let's transport something." Not so long ago it often meant getting around by horse and buggy—if the weather wasn't too bad and, more important, if the roads were in good shape.

Our modern way of life has not only changed the means of transportation, but it has also made it possible to travel easily to distant places and to transport enormous weights by rail, ship and air.

Why Do Wheels Make Work Easier?

You will use:

Shoebox
Three round pencils
String
Several books
Spring scale

Do this:

Attach the string to the box so that you can pull it. Place several books inside the box.

Attach the spring scale to the string. Pull the box.

How much did the scale measure? Write it down.

Place three round pencils under the box. Pull the box.

How much did the scale measure?

Compare your results.

Which rolled easier? Why?

Why it works:

Round objects, such as rollers and wheels, make moving easier than pulling flat objects. This is because there is less friction between a round object and the surface it is rolling on.

Wheels offer even less resistance than rollers.

Let's see if we can begin to understand how jet planes work.

Round supports reduce friction and make the movement of heavy articles easier.

How Do Jet Planes Work?

You will use:

Plastic boat
Medicine dropper
Balloon
Rubber band

Do this:

Remove the rubber part of the medicine dropper.

Place the wide end of the glass medicine dropper about 1 inch into the neck of the balloon. Secure it firmly with a rubber band.

Place a balloon in a toy rowboat. The principle of jet propulsion can be demonstrated in a bathtub of water.

Carefully punch a hole in the rear of the boat. Insert the dropper so that it emerges outside the boat.

Place some water in a bathtub.

Blow up the balloon through the medicine dropper. Hold your finger over the opening, and place the boat in the tub. What happens?

Now take your finger off the opening. In which direction does the boat go?

Why it works:

The air inside a closed balloon pushes evenly in all directions. Therefore, the balloon is not forced to move in any direction.

When the balloon is opened, air rushes out the opening. Since the pressure at this end is being reduced, the pressure at the opposite end causes the balloon to move in that direction. Therefore, as the air escapes to the rear, the balloon and the boat move forward through the water.

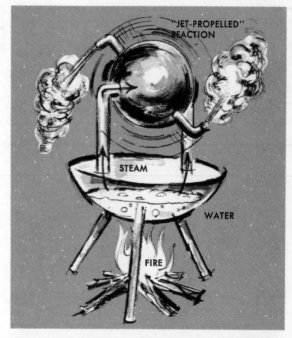

Hero of Alexandria, a Greek scientist who lived about 2,000 years ago, was the first man to demonstrate the principle of jet propulsion. He built a kind of engine as shown above. Fire boiled the water which sent steam through two pipes connected to a hollow ball. Two smaller pipes attached to the ball released the steam, propelling the hollow sphere.

People often ask, "Is jet power something new?" It isn't.

For example, we know that Hero, a

The action of a jet plane can be shown in this experiment which you can make with a balloon. Blow up a balloon. Then release it. A fast stream of air rushes from the neck of the balloon. But the balloon will move in the opposite direction of the stream of air.

Greek scientist and writer who lived in Alexandria, Egypt, about 150 B.C., demonstrated jet action with steam.

First of all, when water boils — or, as scientists say, reaches the boiling point of 212 degrees Fahrenheit — it begins to change into steam — that is, the molecules of water get energy from the heat source and begin to spread out. They move rapidly in all directions. These tiny molecules of water, having gotten a lot of energy from the heat,

really push hard to escape. The escaping molecules form the vapor called steam.

Have you ever listened to a whistling teakettle? It's the steam that blows the whistle.

When steam is put under pressure, it can do a lot of work. Scientists have even measured how much steam we can get from a certain amount of water. For example, one cubic inch of water, when heated to the boiling point, makes about one cubic foot of steam.

How would you like to make a simple steam turbine and see exactly how it works?

How Does a Steam Engine Work?

You will use:

Empty coffee can
4 by 4 inch piece of aluminum foil
Pin
Cork
Hammer
Thin nail
Pencil with eraser
Scissors

Do this:

Hammer the nail into the cover of the can, about 1 inch from the edge, to make a hole.

Make a pinwheel from the aluminum foil. Cut each corner to about ½ inch of the center.

Pin every other corner through the center.

Place the pin through the eraser of your pencil.

Test your pinwheel by blowing on it or by waving it through the air.

Press the sharpened end of the pencil into the cork.

Nail or glue the cork to the center of the coffee-can cover, so that the blades of the pinwheel are above the hole in the cover.

Put a little water in the can. Put on the cover, and place the can on the range.

Soon the pinwheel will begin to spin.

Why it works:

When the water begins to boil, it changes into steam and rushes through the small opening at the top of the can.

The force of the steam pushes against the blades of the pinwheel and turns it.

On a large scale, the steam can do much more work. The more heat applied, the more steam we get.

The steam engine replaced lesser sources of energy, and people began moving about more.

Robert Fulton used steam to enable

ships to travel under their own power. No longer did ships have to depend upon favorable winds to give them power. Burning wood or coal produced the steam to send the ships on their way.

If steam power was such a terrific advance, you may imagine how important the invention of the gasoline engine was.

Ask your Dad to open the hood of

Without the steam engine (cutaway, left), we would have had to rely on the wind to move ships, and horses to pull our trains during those early days.

Later on, the invention of the gasoline engine, or internal combustion machine, greatly increased our transportation possibilities, making travel easier and faster. The use of atomic power will further these possibilities.

his car and let you look inside. The gasoline engine of an automobile works on the principle of internal combustion —that is, explosions take place inside cylinders in the engine block. Each explosion is caused when gasoline vapor mixed with air is ignited by a spark from the spark plug.

The explosion forces the piston inside the cylinder to go down and turn the crankshaft.

We hope that now you are beginning to understand what an internal combustion engine is.

We also hope that you are beginning to understand what is meant when people say that the world has become smaller. Today we can get from one place to another much faster and with much less trouble than people were ever able to do in the past.

Imagine how much easier it will be to travel when atomic power is used in planes, trains, and even automobiles.

The Vegetable Kingdom — Plants

Important Words

Chlorophyll: The green coloring of plants.

Erosion: The wearing-away of the land.

Photosynthesis: The process used by green plants to manufacture their own food.

Pollen: Yellow dust produced by stamens. The pollen helps form new seeds in the plants.

Stomata: Tiny openings in the leaf of a plant, through which oxygen and carbon dioxide pass.

Someone once said that without plants it would be impossible for anything to live on earth.

Let's trace the history of a hamburger or a steak to find out if that's true. It comes from a steer. The steer cannot exist without grass—a plant. What about bread? It is made from a plant —wheat. What about eggs? They come from an animal that depends upon plants for food. What about sugar? That was originally from a plant. Honey would not be made if bees could not get pollen from plants. We could trace back any food this way. It all comes down to this: No plants—no life.

Let's begin by finding out how a plant takes care of itself by manufacturing its own food in its own factory. We know that an animal has to be fed.

Someone must give it food or else it roams around in search of it. We humans have our food prepared for us. It is not so with plants.

Did you ever see how a furniture factory operates? For one thing, you see trucks carrying raw materials— such as planks of lumber, cans of varnish and paint, and kegs of nails— which get unloaded on the platforms. Then you see other trucks carrying finished products—such as chairs and tables—neatly packed and ready for sale, pulling away from the loading platforms of the factory.

The plant factory does not have trucks delivering its raw materials. These materials are carbon dioxide, water, and sunlight. Once the plant has these materials, it goes into operation. The leaf of the plant takes in two of these raw materials—carbon dioxide and sunlight—while water is taken in through the roots. The leaf has tiny openings called stomata. If you look at a section of a leaf under a microscope, you can see these openings.

Leaves "inhale" carbon dioxide and "exhale" oxygen through small holes called stomata (enlarged).

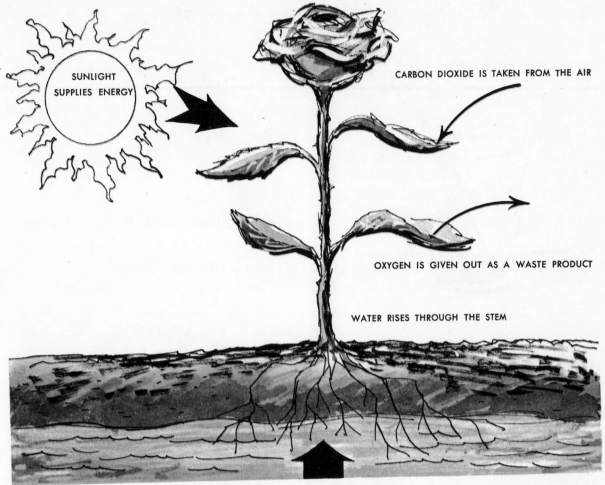

SUNLIGHT SUPPLIES ENERGY

CARBON DIOXIDE IS TAKEN FROM THE AIR

OXYGEN IS GIVEN OUT AS A WASTE PRODUCT

WATER RISES THROUGH THE STEM

WATER IS TAKEN OUT BY THE ROOTS

After the openings take in the raw materials, chemical changes take place. The raw materials—carbon dioxide, water, and sun—go to work on the tiny bits of matter inside the leaf. These bits of matter give the plant its green color and are called chlorophyll. The result of this work is the manufacture of starch. In the process, oxygen is given off.

The sugar is used in all parts of the plant to help it live and grow.

This making of food has a name we should know. It is called photosynthesis.

That is quite a word. What does it mean? Let's take the word apart and see. You've heard of "photo"—it means "light." "Synthesis" means "building up" or "putting together." The whole word means "putting together under the influence of light."

Plants don't depend upon their leaves for water. Instead, they get water from the earth through a special tube system of roots and root hairs. Roots do more than get moisture and minerals for the food-making of a plant. In addition, they serve as anchors. Like a ship, they have to be anchored so that they don't drift off as a result of wind and rain. The roots hold the soil together and prevent what we call erosion, or the wearing away of the soil.

How Can You Change the Color of a Leaf?

You will use:

Drinking glass
Celery stalk
Red ink
Water

Do this:

Add red ink to a half-glass of water. Place a celery stalk in the glass. Leave it there for several hours.

The leaves should become red.

Cut the stem crosswise in several places to see the tubes that carried the water to the leaves.

Cross section of a stem showing the tubes, or canals.

Why it works:

As the colored water wets the inside of the tiny tubes in the celery, they draw the water up higher than the level of water in the glass. This is called capillary action.

A more interesting experiment can be made in which a white flower is given two different colors. Split the stalk of a white flower in half and place each end of the stalk in a separate glass of water, each of a different color. After some time has elapsed, you will notice that one half of the flower is of one color, and the other half is of another color.

Do Green Plants Need Sunlight?

You will use:

Two similar potted plants
One large box to serve as a cover

Do this:

Cover one plant with the large box. Make several holes in the box to let air in.
Water both plants daily.

What will happen?

After several days, compare the healthy, green, uncovered plant with the one that was covered.

The covered plant will probably be yellowed and frail.

Sunlight was kept from the plant. It did not have the opportunity to manufacture its own food. The plant suffered from "malnutrition."

Try to revive the plant by placing it in the sun.

Do Plants Bend Toward the Sun?

You will use:

Green plant
Large corrugated box

Do this:

Make an opening in the side of the box at about the height the leaves will reach when placed inside.

Place the plant in the box. Have the opening of the box directly in the path of the sun.

What will happen?

After several hours the leaves and stems are bent toward the light of the sun.

Turn the plant so the leaves point away from the opening. After several more hours they will again turn toward the light.

Again we see that green plants need sunlight and grow toward it.

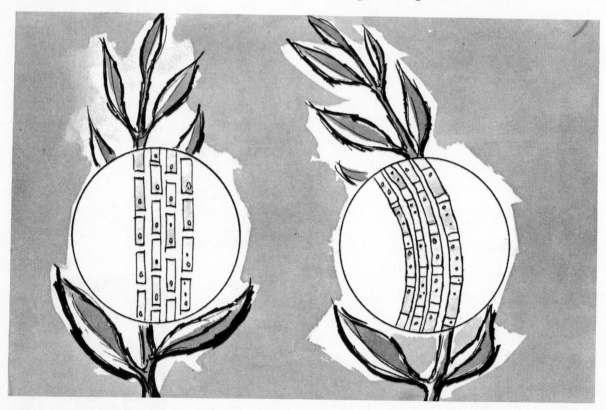

When a plant is growing straight up, an examination of its cells would show that they were about uniform in size. However, when the plant cells on one side grow larger than the cells on the other side, the plant will bend.

Do Green Plants Need Water?

You will use:

Two similar potted plants

Do this:

Place both flowerpots in the sunlight.
Water one plant daily. Do not water the other.
Label each pot accordingly.

What will happen?

After several days, notice that one plant is thriving while the other is wilted and dying.

Water, which is necessary for photosynthesis, was kept from one plant. The plant was unable to manufacture its food and began to die.

Try to revive it by watering it.

A plant that has enough water grows.

Without enough water a plant will wither.

Do Green Plants Need Air?

You will use:

Two similar potted plants
Large jar
Two small dishes of water

Do this:

Place each flowerpot in a small dish of water.
Cover one plant with a jar.
Press the jar into the soil so that no air can reach the plant.
Place both plants in sunlight.

What will happen?

Observe what happens after several days.

The plant getting the air will show great vitality and life.

We have seen so far that plants need light, water, and air.

All plants "breathe." Without air they would die.

FLOATING

EXPLODING

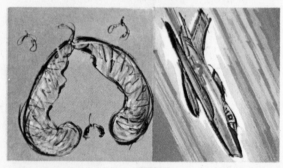

FLYING

STICKING

HITCHHIKING

So far, we have only been considering half the story. We have learned about leaves and roots but not about flowers and stems.

Do you remember why we said that leaves and roots are important? Leaves help the plant make food for itself. And roots and root hairs help to bring moisture and minerals to feed the plant.

Now, the flower's job is to help the plant produce more plants. Here's how it happens.

Look at this tulip. Those flat lollipop-shaped objects inside the petals are called stamens. Squeeze the tip. Do you see the yellow powder? That's called pollen. When an insect visits a flower, some of the pollen sticks to its body and legs. This pollen drops off as the insect goes to another flower. Sometimes wind blows pollen from flower to flower. If the pollen falls on the sticky, vase-shaped part of the flower called the pistil, it makes its way down to the egg cells where the seeds are fertilized. When the seeds ripen, they may grow into new plants.

Look at the seeds the next time you eat an apple. If you throw the core into the garden, do you think an apple tree will grow?

It might. Some plants have interesting ways of scattering seeds that parachute to earth. Others are exploded into the air. Some fly or glide. There are seeds that stick to animals and still others that are scattered by birds.

You may not have realized that a plant is so complicated. And we haven't

Seeds, almost like the actions of men, it seems, can float, explode, fly in the air, stick, and are carried away. These are the ways seeds are scattered about.

A TYPICAL GREEN PLANT

Cross section through a flower

mentioned another use for seeds. We eat seeds. Think of stringbeans and peas. Rice is a most wonderful seed. A great part of the population of the world eats rice as its main food. We eat wheat, corn, barley, cereals—like oats. Why, we even get oils from seeds —from corn, cotton, peanuts and sunflowers.

We also eat the leaves of plants, such as lettuce and cabbage. And when we eat cauliflower, we're eating the flower of the plant. And we also eat stems, such as asparagus and celery.

We also benefit from other parts of plants and trees. We get paper from wood pulp, as well as wood for toys, furniture and houses.

The sap of a tree is also important. You know the syrup your mother serves with wheatcakes for breakfast? Yes, that's part of the sap of a tree.

Here's a problem. The automobile would never be as popular as it is today if it were not for trees. Why?

The answer is that the juice from some trees gives the raw rubber for our tires.

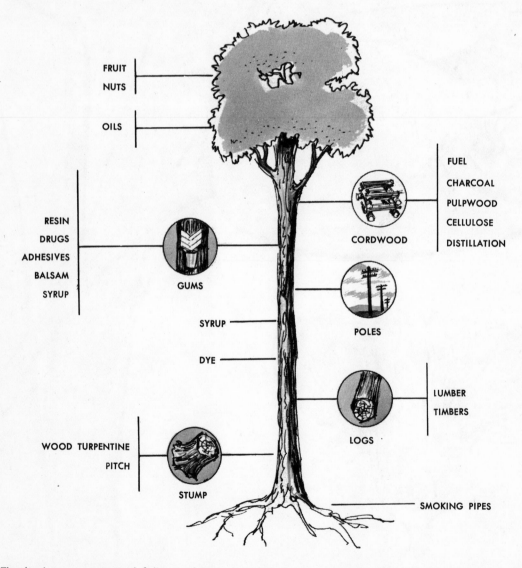

The bark, sap, roots and foliage of trees have given man several useful products for home and industry.

Can You See Seeds Grow?

You will use:

Olive jar
Absorbent cotton
Seeds, such as pumpkin, lima bean, corn, pea

Do this:

Fill the olive jar with cotton.

Place seeds between the cotton and the glass.

Do not place seeds too close to each other.

Wet the cotton and keep it damp for several days.

What will happen?

After several days the shoots or stems will be growing upward and the roots will be growing downward.

Invert the glass.

After several more days the stems and roots will turn so that again the stems grow up and the roots grow down.

If the seeds continue growing in the glass for several days, you will notice that they appear to be dying. Why do you think this happens? The plants seem to be getting everything they need for photosynthesis—carbon dioxide, water, and sunlight. But they are missing some minerals that are found in soil. Up to this point, each plant was living off itself. It was getting its nourishment from the food stored in the seed. Now that it is ready to manufacture its own food, it should have these minerals.

You can revive the plants by placing them in flowerpots with soil.

The shoots grow upward and the roots downward.

Inverted glass: Shoots still grow up, roots down.

47

Some Famous Men of Science

Luther Burbank (1849-1926), American, plant scientist who developed many new varieties of plant.

George Washington Carver (1864-1943), American, botanist and chemist who found many uses for peanuts, sweet potatoes, and soybeans.

Thomas Alva Edison (1847-1931), American, inventor of the electric light bulb.

Michael Faraday (1791-1867), English, made the first electric generator.

Henry Ford (1863-1947), American, pioneer in the development of the automobile and its manufacture.

Robert Fulton (1765-1815), American, inventor of the first commercially successful steamboat.

James Clerk-Maxwell (1831-1879), Scot, formulated theories of light.

Albert Abraham Michelson (1852-1931), American, determined the speed of light.

Isaac Newton (1642-1727), English, scientist and mathematician; among his many achievements was his work in the fields of gravity and motion.

Max Planck (1858-1947), German, Nobel Prize winner for his theory of light.

Charles Proteus Steinmetz (1865-1923), American, made many contributions in the field of electrical engineering.

Evangelista Torricelli (1608-1647), Italian, invented the barometer.

Alessandro Volta (1745-1827), Italian, made the first battery that produced an electric current.

Orville Wright (1871-1948) and Wilbur Wright (1867-1912), American, pioneers in the invention and development of the airplane.

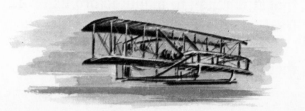

THE HOW AND WHY WONDER BOOK OF
SCIENCE EXPERIMENTS

Written by MARTIN L. KEEN
Illustrated by GEORGE J. ZAFFO
Editorial Production: DONALD D. WOLF

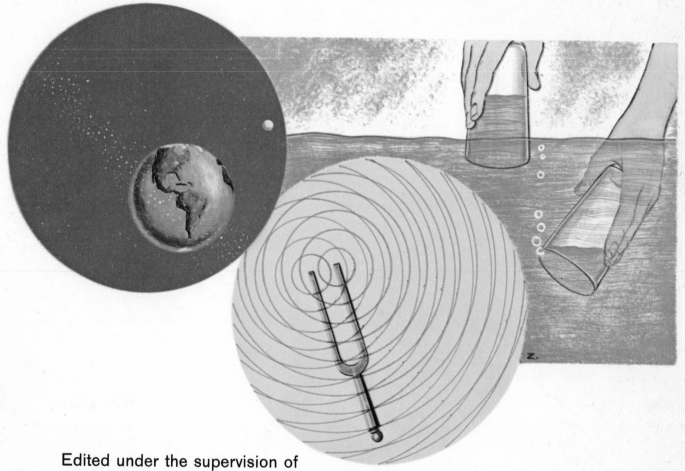

Edited under the supervision of
  Dr. Paul E. Blackwood
  Washington, D. C.

Text and illustrations approved by
  Oakes A. White, Brooklyn Children's Museum, Brooklyn, New York

GROSSET & DUNLAP • Publishers • NEW YORK

Introduction

The experiment is one of the scientist's ways of discovering new knowledge about the relationships of events in nature. Through experimenting, scientists can check on their speculations, their hunches, their guesses and their guiding ideas about what causes things to happen the way they do.

The How and Why Wonder Book of Science Experiments provides suggested investigations in three very important areas of exploration — air and water, sound, and astronomy. By making these investigations, each young explorer will be rediscovering some of the principles of science. But in some of the activities, new knowledge will be discovered. For example, counting the meteors that appear at a certain time in a part of the sky will supply new facts — facts not known to anyone else. This is a real discovery. If reported properly, the facts may help astronomers refine the present knowledge about meteors.

This book shows that the study of different things in the world may require different techniques and tools — vibrating strings to study sound waves, scales and thermometers to study the air and water, telescopes and field glasses to study the stars. But they all require some of the same habits of careful investigation, such as keen observation, good thinking, accurate record keeping and painstaking experimentation.

Thus, *The How and Why Wonder Book of Science Experiments* will be a helpful guide to assist young scientists at home and at school to explore interesting phases of knowledge. It will help them to develop skills of investigation through using the methods of discovery that experienced scientists use.

Paul E. Blackwood

Dr. Blackwood is a professional employee in the U. S. Office of Education. This book was edited by him in his private capacity and no official support or endorsement by the Office of Education is intended or should be inferred.

Contents

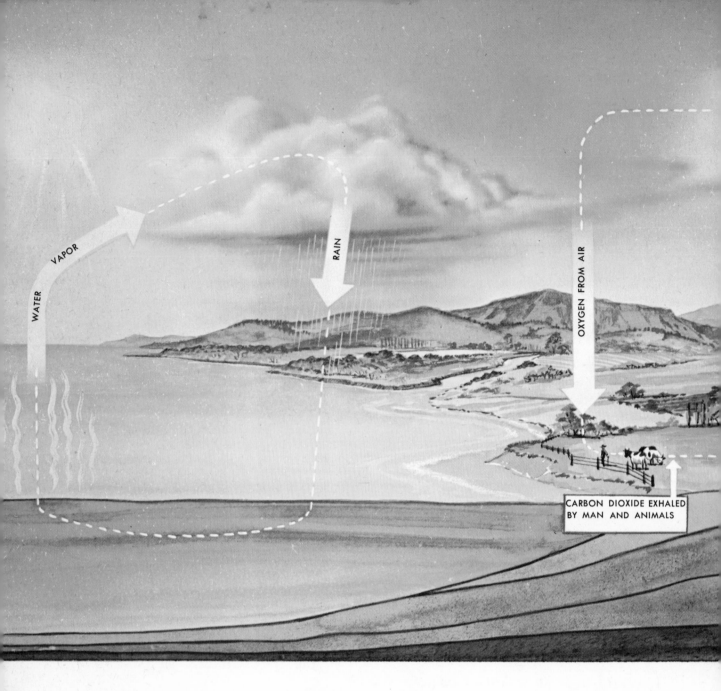

WATER VAPOR

RAIN

OXYGEN FROM AIR

CARBON DIOXIDE EXHALED BY MAN AND ANIMALS

Air and Water

Air and water are two materials with which everyone is familiar. We live at the bottom of an ocean of air, called the atmosphere. Air surrounds our bodies every minute of our lives, except when we are swimming or bathing. Air may be found in almost every open hollow in all materials on the surface of the earth. There is air also in many of the hollows and openings of the human body — for example, our ears, mouth, nose, and lungs. All animals breath air, and if deprived of it, they die.

The waters of seas, lakes, rivers, and streams cover three-quarters of the earth's surface. Water is necessary for life. The cells of which all living things are made are largely water. Water, given enough time, will dissolve almost any substance. This is important, be-

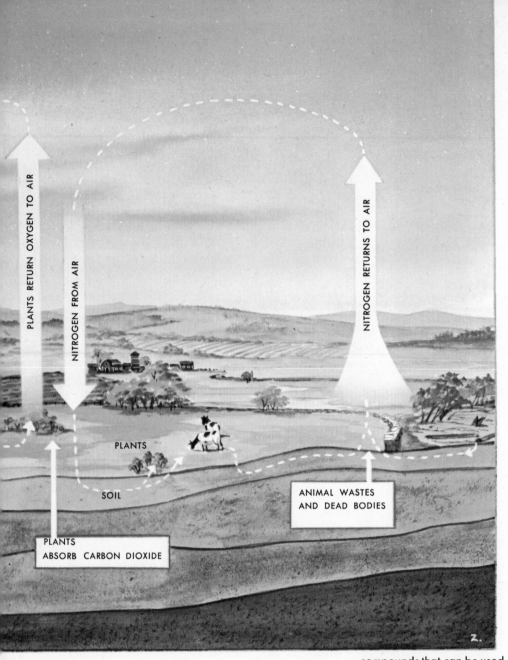

PLANTS RETURN OXYGEN TO AIR

NITROGEN FROM AIR

NITROGEN RETURNS TO AIR

PLANTS

SOIL

ANIMAL WASTES
AND DEAD BODIES

PLANTS
ABSORB CARBON DIOXIDE

ONE-CELLED PROTOZOA

ONE-CELLED ALGAE

The two major gases, nitrogen and oxygen, continually leave and then return to the atmosphere in endless processes, or cycles. Nitrogen from the air that penetrates the upper layers of the soil is changed by certain bacteria to chemical compounds that can be used as nourishment by plants. The plants may be eaten by animals that excrete compounds of nitrogen, which are decomposed by other bacteria, releasing nitrogen to the air. Dead plants and animals, too, are decomposed by bacteria in a process that eventually releases nitrogen to the air. The released nitrogen now may re-enter the soil — as the nitrogen cycle continues, over and over again. Oxygen is breathed by animals that exhale carbon dioxide. Plants absorb carbon dioxide from the air and give off oxygen that is again breathed by animals — as the oxygen cycle continues endlessly. Water falls from clouds as rain or snow. The fallen water forms streams and rivers that run into lakes and oceans. The heat of the sun evaporates water from these natural bodies of water. The evaporated water rises into the air as water vapor that cools to form clouds that produce more rain.

cause the materials that nourish living things are dissolved in water. This water makes up the main part of the blood of animals and the sap of plants, the two fluids that carry nourishing materials to the cells of living things.

We shall perform experiments concerning both air and water, because, as we shall see, these two materials are closely connected in many ways.

The bubbles are air that was held in the spaces between the particles of earth and freed when the earth was submerged in water.

Gently drop a clod of earth into a pot or glass full of water.

How can you show that some materials hold air?

Note the bubbles that arise. These bubbles are air that was held in the spaces between the particles of earth. The fact that air can penetrate into the soil is very important to the growth of plants. Probably the most needed substance for plant nourishment is the chemical element nitrogen. Four-fifths of air is nitrogen. Yet plants cannot obtain nitrogen directly from the air. However, certain bacteria that live in the soil can remove nitrogen from the air and change the nitrogen to a form that can be used by plants. Thus, you can see why it is important that air penetrates soil.

Into some clean water put a piece of brick and a smooth, well-washed pebble. Note that air bubbles arise from the piece of brick, but not from the pebble. There are many air spaces in brick, but none in solid stone. This shows that not all substances are penetrated by air.

BRICK

PEBBLE

Air is trapped only in the brick, not the pebble.

Place a clean glass of water in the sun. Look at it about an hour later. Do you see the bubbles on the inside of the glass? They are air bubbles. Pour the water from the glass into a pot, set the pot on a stove, and boil the water. Now, many more bubbles arise from the water, showing that more air was in the water. You cannot boil all the air out of the water, because more is entering the water as you boil some out.

The bubbles on the inside of the glass of water in the sun are air bubbles.

If you boil the water, more air boils out.

If we have a box in which we cannot see anything, we say that the box is empty. After we have drunk all the water in a glass, we say that there

How can you prove that air is really a kind of matter?

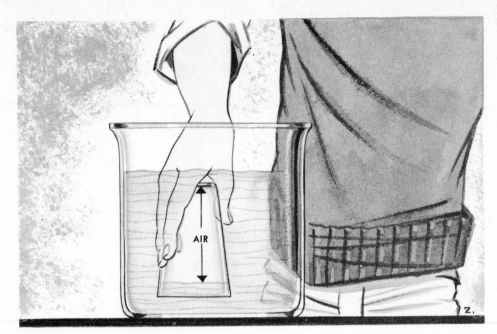

The air that occupies the space in the glass prevents the water from pushing up all the way in the glass.

is nothing in the glass. Yet, it is not true that there is nothing in the box and glass — both are full of air. Although we cannot see air, we must not believe that air is nothing at all. Air is matter. Like all matter, it takes up space and has weight.

Lower a drinking glass, mouth downward, into a large jar or pot three-quarters full of water. Note that the water pushes only a little way up into the glass. What keeps the water from rising all the way up into the glass? Something must be taking up the space inside the glass and thereby keeping the water out. It is air that occupies the space in the glass.

Obtain two balloons of the same size. Blow them up to the same size, and tie their necks so that the air will not escape. After tying each balloon, leave about a foot-and-a-half of string free, and tie a loop at the end of each string.

Tie a string around the middle of a yardstick, and suspend it so that it swings freely. Slip the loops at the ends of the strings that are attached to the balloons over the ends of the yardstick, and adjust the balloons so that they balance the yardstick. When the yardstick has stopped swinging, burst one of the balloons with a pin. The other balloon will swing downward. Since both the full balloon and the burst balloon weigh the same, there must be something on the side of the full balloon that pulls the yardstick down on that side. This something is the air in the balloon. This proves that air has weight.

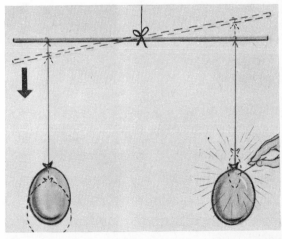

You can actually demonstrate that air has weight.

7

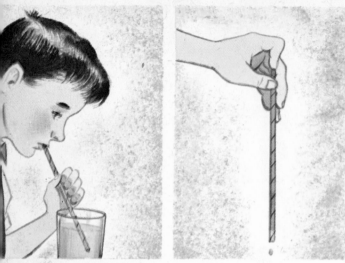
Atmospheric pressure holds water in the straw.

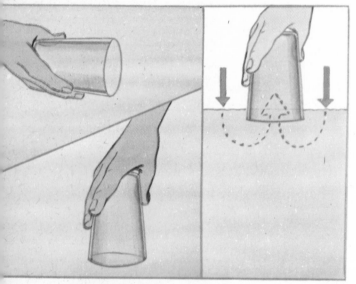
Atmospheric pressure holds the water in the glass.

This means that the atmosphere presses on every inch of the earth's surface with a weight of nearly fifteen pounds. It is this weight that we mean when we speak of atmospheric pressure.

Atmosphere exerts its pressure not only straight downward, but equally in all directions. The pressure of the air on the body of a human being is several tons. Why doesn't this great pressure crush us? It is because the air that enters the body through the mouth and nose, and the air that is in the water of all our cells, is pushing outward with as much pressure as is pushing inward. Because of this balance of pressure, we feel no pressure at all.

The atmosphere extends 600 miles above the earth's surface. One-quarter of the atmosphere is within one-and-a-half miles of the surface, half within three-and-a-half miles, and ninety-nine one-hundredths within twenty miles. The total weight of the earth's atmosphere is one million billion tons. A column of the atmosphere one inch square and 600 miles high weighs nearly fifteen pounds.

What is atmospheric pressure?

8

How can we demonstrate atmospheric pressure? Fill a drinking straw with water, and place your finger tightly over one end. Turn the straw so that the open end points downward. Some water will run out, but most will remain in the straw. What keeps most of the water from running out? It is the atmospheric pressure that is pressing upward at almost fifteen pounds per square inch.

Run enough water into a sink or large jar so that you can place a glass on its side completely under water. Keeping the glass under water, turn it around so that its mouth points downward. Raise the glass, until all but about half an inch of it is out of the water. The glass remains full of water, even though it is upside down. What keeps the water in the glass? Atmospheric pressure on the surface of the water in the sink or jar pushes water up into the glass. The weight of the air on the surface of the water in the sink or jar is greater than the weight of the water in the glass. Thus the water is held inside the glass at a level higher than the surface of the water outside the glass.

The experiments you just performed are somewhat like one performed by the Italian physicist E. Torricelli (1608-1647). He filled a long glass tube with water. The tube was nearly forty feet long and had a faucet at one end; the other end was closed. Torricelli stood the glass tube upright in a tub of water, the faucet end down. He then opened the faucet. Some of the water ran out the bottom of the tube. The length of the column of water that was left was thirty-four feet. Torricelli knew, then, the pressure of air on the water in the tub was enough to support a column of water thirty-four feet high. He weighed the water in the tube and from this weight he was able to calculate that, in order to hold up a column of water thirty-four feet high, the atmosphere had to press downward with a weight of nearly fifteen pounds per square inch. In this way, Torricelli was the first to discover exactly what atmospheric pressure is. Torricelli performed his experiment at sea level. If he had performed it on top of Mount Everest, which is approximately six miles high, there would have been less air above the tub

Torricelli, at the beginning of the seventeenth century, discovered the nature of atmospheric pressure.

Changes of air pressure are measured by a barometer. A mercurial barometer consists of a column of mercury in a glass tube about 35 inches high. As the pressure of the atmosphere changes, the column of mercury rises and falls. An aneroid barometer consists of a tightly-sealed can from which some air has been removed. A pointer is soldered to a pivot at the top of the can. As the pressure of air changes, the top of the can moves in or out, thus moving the pointer over a scale on which changes in pressure may be read.

ANEROID BAROMETER

MERCURY BAROMETER

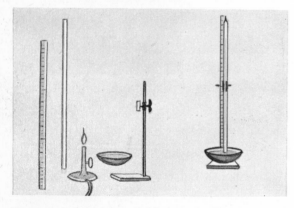

You can make a mercurial barometer in your school laboratory. Obtain a glass tube about 35 inches long. Place one end of the tube into a hot flame, such as that of a Bunsen burner. Twirl the tube around until the end melts and is sealed. When the tube has cooled, fill it to the top with mercury. Also, fill a dessert dish or beaker with mercury. Hold your finger over the open end of the tube and carefully invert it, placing the open end beneath the surface of the mercury in the dish. Place a yardstick alongside the glass tube and clamp both upright. Changes in pressure may be read on the yardstick as the height of the mercury in the tube changes.

to press on the surface of the water. As a result, he would have found atmospheric pressure to be only a little more than six pounds per square inch.

A siphon is a tube in the form of an inverted U, through which liquids flow over the walls of a container, due to atmospheric pressure. To make a siphon, obtain a rubber or plastic tube, about three feet long and not more than half an inch wide. You will also need two water pails, or other deep vessels. Fill one pail three-quarters full of water, and place it in a sink. Place the other pail on the floor, almost directly below the pail in the sink.

How can you make a siphon?

Hold one end of the tube in each hand and completely fill the tube with water from the faucet. Place your fingers over the ends of the tube, so that no water can escape. Quickly place one end well below the surface of the water in the pail in the sink. Let the other end of the tube hang down above the pail on the floor. This end of the tube must be lower than the end in the water. Remove your fingers from both ends of the tube at the same time. You will find that water flows through the tube, over the top of the pail in the sink, and down to the pail on the floor. The operation you have just performed takes some skill, so that you may have to try it more than once, but it is not really difficult.

Why does water flow over the edge of the pail? Because, when you removed your finger from the lower end of the tube, some water fell out, just as it did from the drinking straw in your first experiment on atmospheric pressure.

How to make your own siphon.

Obtain a cork that fits tightly into the neck of a soda bottle. (A one-hole rubber stopper will work even better than a cork.) Bore a narrow hole through the cork. Into this hole, push the glass tube from an eye dropper. Be sure that the tube fits the hole tightly. If it does not, seal it into the hole with rubber cement, modeling clay, or putty. Using a length of rubber tubing, attach to the wide end of the eye dropper tube a length of glass tubing that reaches nearly to the bottom of the bottle. Fill the bottle about one-fourth full of water. Lower the glass-tube assembly into the bottle and press the cork tightly in. Hold the cork with your fingers, and blow hard into the bottle in order to compress the air within. Quickly point the bottle away from you, and watch a stream of water gush from the tip of the eye dropper tube.

The water that fell out of the tube left an empty space behind it. Atmospheric pressure on the surface of water in the pail pushed water up into the tube to fill the empty space. More water fell out of the bottom of the tube, and was again replaced, due to atmospheric pressure — and the water continued to flow through the siphon tube.

In 1654, a German scientist, Otto von

How can you demonstrate the force of air pressure?

Guericke, amazed everyone by showing how much force could be exerted by the pressure of the atmosphere. He used two iron hemispheres, each of which was about twenty-two inches in diameter. Their rims were carefully ground smooth and covered with grease. He put the rims together, and, with a vacuum pump he had invented, removed the air inside the hollow sphere. So great was the air pressure on the outside that it took sixteen horses, eight on each side, to pull the hemispheres apart.

You can perform an experiment like that of von Guericke. You will need two plungers of the kind that are used to force water through drains. You will also need a friend to help you. Thoroughly wet both plungers. Ask your friend to sit in a chair and hold the

plunger handle between his knees, the rubber cup upward. Place the cup of your plunger upon the other one, and slowly and carefully push down until most of the air has been expelled from the plunger cups. Now, each of you grasp a handle, and see how difficult it is to pull the plungers apart.

If you have only one plunger, place it on a smooth wet surface, and push down hard. You will see how strongly you have to pull in order to pull it free. All the force holding the plunger to the surface is due to atmospheric pressure.

How does atmospheric pressure help us breathe?

When we take a breath, air enters our lungs. People usually say that we "draw" air into our lungs, but this is not an accurate way to describe what happens. Let us see how we breathe. Our lungs are two large sacs of membrane suspended within the cage of our ribs. The lungs have no muscles, and therefore we have no direct control over them. Below our lungs is a large curved muscle, called the *diaphragm*. To take a breath, we pull the top of this muscle downward. Doing this raises our ribs

Sixteen horses were not able to pull the steel spheres apart after the German scientist Otto von Guericke had removed the air between the spheres. This occurred in 1654 in Magdeburg. Try to separate two plungers and you will see how difficult it can be.

and makes more room within the rib cage. The lungs now have room to expand. The air pressure outside the lungs is greater than the air pressure within the lungs, so air is pushed into the lungs from outside our body. This is the act of inhaling.

To exhale, we relax the diaphragm, thereby lowering the rib cage, which presses the air out of the lungs.

To make a model of our breathing apparatus, we need a bell jar — a bell-shaped glass that is open at the bottom. We also need a one-hole rubber stopper that will fit the neck of the bell jar,

a glass tube in the shape of a Y, two small balloons, and a large thin piece of rubber.

Place the stopper in the mouth of the jar. Tie the two balloons to the ends of the arms of the Y-tube. Put the other end of the Y-tube into the hole in the stopper, doing so by way of the bottom of the bell jar. Tie the large piece of rubber around the bottom of the bell jar.

The large piece of rubber represents the diaphragm. The upper part of the Y-tube represents the trachea, the arms represent the bronchial tubes, and the balloons represent the lungs. By pulling

13

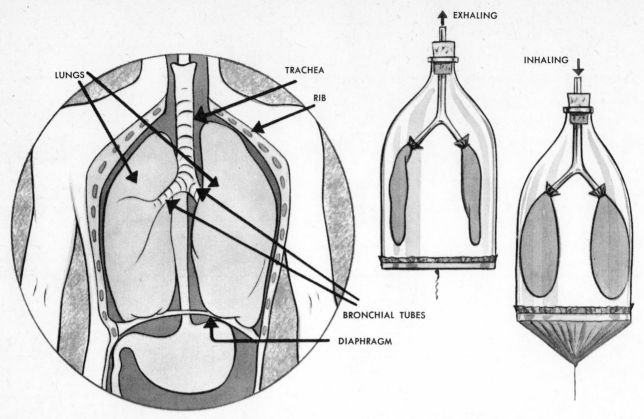

LUNGS

TRACHEA

RIB

BRONCHIAL TUBES

DIAPHRAGM

EXHALING

INHALING

How we breath (at left) and how you can simulate the process of breathing.

down on the rubber diaphragm, you simulate the act of inhaling. Then, by pushing upward on the diaphragm, you simulate exhaling.

A Cartesian diver is a toy that depends on two principles: The first is that air is elastic, and the second is that air is lighter than water. You can easily prove that air is elastic by holding a finger tightly over the outlet of a tire pump. Push the plunger in, and suddenly let go. The plunger springs back as if it had been pushed into rubber, which, as you know, is very elastic.

How can you make Cartesian divers?

That air is lighter than water is proved by the fact that air bubbles rise in water. Lighter materials rise to the top of heavier ones. Thus, air is lighter than water.

A real Cartesian diver is a tiny figure of a man made of some material that is a little heavier than water. Inside this figure is a small glass tube, closed at one end, and with the open end pointing downward. The whole apparatus is made of materials of such weight that it floats just below the surface of the water. The Cartesian diver is put into a tall jar filled with water to the very top, and covered by a thin piece of rubber. When you press down on the rubber, the water transmits your push to the air in the glass tube inside the diver. The air, being elastic, is compressed, so that it occupies a smaller space. The result is that the air is less able to hold up the diver, which sinks toward the bottom of the jar. By giving the rubber just the right amount of push, you can make the diver rise and sink, or float at any level you wish.

14

It is quite difficult to make a real Cartesian diver, but we can have much fun with substitute divers. Our divers will be paper matches cut in half, the half with the matchheads attached being used. We place three or four of our divers into a bottle with a very thin neck, one over which you can easily place your thumb. Fill the bottle with water to the very top. The half matches will float because of air within the fibers of the paper.

Put your thumb over the top of the bottle, and press downward. This will compress the air in the half matches, and their heavy heads will pull them down to the bottom. When you release the pressure of your thumb, the divers will rise. With a little practice, you can make your divers sink and rise and float at whatever level you wish.

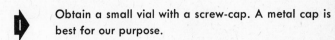
Obtain a small vial with a screw-cap. A metal cap is best for our purpose.

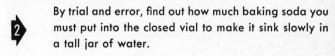
By trial and error, find out how much baking soda you must put into the closed vial to make it sink slowly in a tall jar of water.

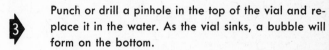
Punch or drill a pinhole in the top of the vial and replace it in the water. As the vial sinks, a bubble will form on the bottom.

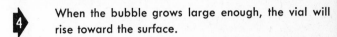
When the bubble grows large enough, the vial will rise toward the surface.

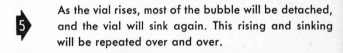
As the vial rises, most of the bubble will be detached, and the vial will sink again. This rising and sinking will be repeated over and over.

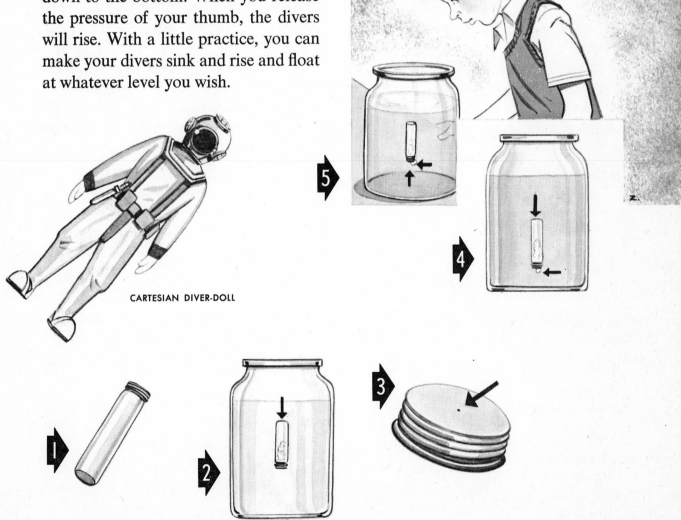

CARTESIAN DIVER-DOLL

15

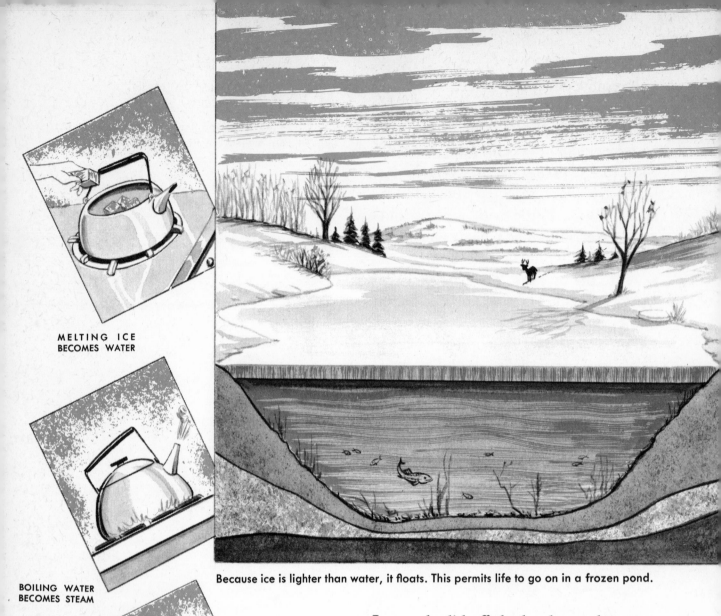

MELTING ICE BECOMES WATER

BOILING WATER BECOMES STEAM

DROPS OF WATER FORM ON THE SPOON

Because ice is lighter than water, it floats. This permits life to go on in a frozen pond.

Water can exist in three different forms, or *states:* solid, liquid, and gas. Put three or four ice cubes in a tea kettle, and put the kettle over a small flame on a stove.

Why aren't fishes frozen in winter ice?

Leave the lid off the kettle, so that you can watch what happens inside. As the ice is heated, it melts and becomes water; it changes from the solid to the liquid state. When all the ice has melted, put the lid on the kettle, and turn the flame up higher. Make sure that the spout is pointing away from you. Soon, the water will boil. You will see steam in front of the spout. Steam is made up of little droplets of water. Look closely at the space just in front of the spout. You will see what looks like an empty space, but the space is taken up by water vapor, which is invisible, because it is colorless. Water vapor is water in the state of a gas. To prove that water vapor is a form of water, wrap a towel around the handle of a tablespoon, and hold the bowl of the spoon in the seemingly empty space in front of the spout. You will see drops of water form on the spoon. If you put these drops of water into the freezer of a refrigerator, they would freeze and become ice.

Water is an unusual substance, because, unlike most other substances, it is lighter in its solid than its liquid state. Ice is lighter than water. When water is cooled to within a few degrees of its freezing point, it suddenly begins to become lighter. It continues to become lighter until it freezes. The fact that ice is lighter is important to all fish, plants, and other forms of life that live in water that freezes in winter. When a pond, lake, or river freezes, the ice floats. This leaves water below, in which fish, water plants, and other living things continue to live almost as they did before the ice formed. If ice were heavier than water, a body of water would freeze from the bottom upward. The water plants would freeze and die. The fish would have shallower and shallower water in which to swim, as the level of ice rose. Finally, the fish would be frozen into the ice as the last water, at the surface, froze. You

have surely seen ice cubes floating in cool drinks. The fact that the ice floats proves it is lighter than water.

Why is ice lighter than water? You can demonstrate why ice is lighter than water by means of the following experiment. Obtain a small screw-cap bottle with a narrow neck and wide shoulders. Fill the bottle to the very top with water, and screw the cap on tightly. Put about two dozen ice cubes into a pail. Add three glassfuls of water. Also add a generous handful of salt. Place the screw-cap bottle into the ice, water mixture, and salt. Stir the mixture frequently. After about fifteen minutes, or more, the water in the bottle will freeze and the bottle will break. If the ice melts before the water in the bottle freezes, add more ice and a little more salt.

Why did the bottle break? It broke because when the water in the bottle froze, it expanded. The ice expanded to take up more room than the water. Since the ice took up more room, it could no longer fit into the bottle, and the force of its expansion broke the bottle.

Suppose you had another bottle the same size as the one that broke, and

When water freezes, it expands. Ice takes more room than water.

suppose that there were some way to put the ice into this bottle. Since the ice takes up more room than the water, you would have some ice left over. Now, if you let the ice in the bottle melt, the water from the melted ice would not fill the bottle. This is true because some of the water originally in the first bottle made up the ice you couldn't put into the second bottle. You can easily see that an amount of water that only partly fills a bottle will weigh less than an amount that completely fills the bottle. The water from the melted ice only partly filled the bottle. This shows that a bottle of ice weighs less than a bottle of water. So, ice weighs less than water.

We learned that water vapor is water in

How can you take water out of air?

the state of a gas. It is not necessary to boil water in order to cause it to become water vapor. At the surface of any body of water, some water is almost always leaving the surface and passing into the air in the form of water vapor. There are tons and tons of water vapor in the atmosphere. Warm air can contain more water vapor than cool air. Air can be cooled to a point at which it can no longer hold all the water vapor it contains. When this happens, the water vapor forms droplets of water. Clouds are made up of droplets of water that has formed from water vapor; so is fog. If clouds are cooled further, their droplets of water form big drops that fall as rain.

Another form in which water vapor leaves the air is dew. At night, leaves, grass, and stones cool more quickly than the air. Air passing over these cool objects is, in its turn, cooled. The cool air cannot hold its water vapor, which leaves the air to form the dew drops so familiar to anyone who goes out early on a summer morning. The temperature at which water vapor becomes water is called the *dew point*.

Nature's water cycle, evaporation, condensation, and precipitation, repeats itself endlessly.

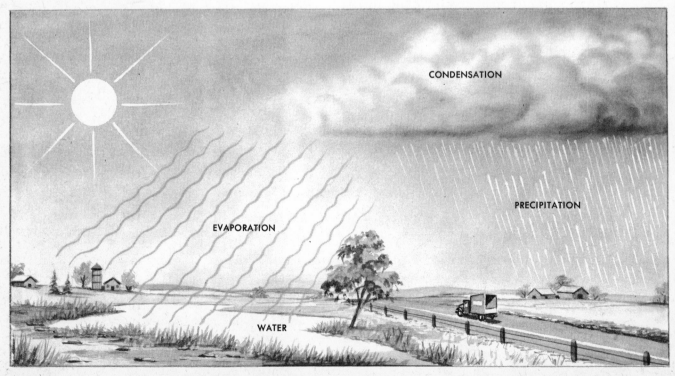

CONDENSATION

PRECIPITATION

EVAPORATION

WATER

As there is always some moisture in the air, the jar will always be moist after the temperature has reached the dew point.

Let us form dew and measure the dew point in the following manner. Put water and some ice cubes into a shiny tin can. Just before putting a thermometer into the can, read the temperature. This is the temperature of the air. Stir the ice and water slowly. Watch the outside of the can carefully. When you see drops of water begin to form on the can, read the thermometer. This temperature is the dew point, and is the temperature of air that is touching the can. Note that this temperature is lower than the temperature of the surrounding air.

Everyone knows that air from an electric fan feels cool on a hot day. We usually take it for granted that the fan is blowing cool air. But if you stop to think about it, you will realize that the air the fan is blowing upon you is the same air that makes you feel uncomfortably warm. Why, then, does this blast of warm air make you feel cool?

Why does an electric fan cool us?

When we heat water so that it turns into water vapor, we say we. are *evapo-*

rating the water. In order to evaporate, the water takes up some of the heat that we apply. Suppose you heat a spoon, and then drop some warm water into it. If the spoon is hot enough, the water will sizzle and dance about in the bowl of the spoon — and evaporate. When this has happened, the spoon will be much cooler. The main reason for this is that the spoon used up much heat in evaporating the water. Thus, you can see that evaporation is a cooling process.

On hot days you perspire, and your perspiration gathers in small drops on your skin, where it slowly evaporates. When a blast of air from a fan strikes

Evaporation is a cooling process.

the perspiration, the rate of evaporation is greatly increased. Since evaporation is a cooling process, the rate of cooling is increased, and the air from the fan causes you to feel cool.

Read the temperature on a thermometer. Put two or three layers of moistened cleansing tissue around the bulb of the thermometer. Place the thermometer in the blast of air of an electric fan. Watch the temperature go down, as evaporation of water from the tissue cools the thermometer's bulb.

THE "MAGIC" BALLOON

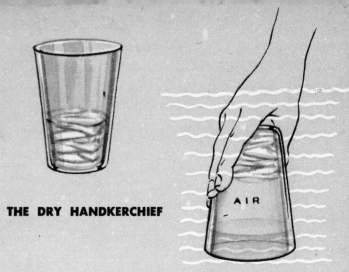

THE DRY HANDKERCHIEF

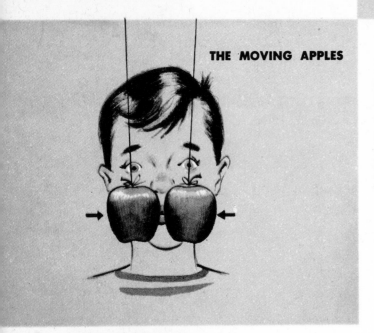

THE MOVING APPLES

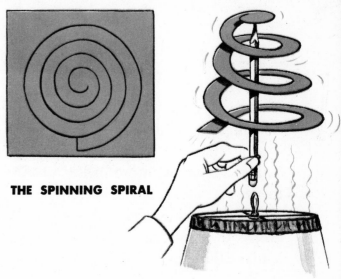

THE SPINNING SPIRAL

THE "MAGIC" BALLOON

Place a soda bottle in a bowl of ice cubes or cracked ice. After a few minutes, when the bottle has become cold, slip a deflated balloon over the neck of the bottle. Remove the bottle from the ice and wait about five minutes until the bottle returns to room temperature. Now place the bottle in a bowl of hot water. The balloon will become inflated as the heat expands the air within the bottle.

THE DRY HANDKERCHIEF

Push a handkerchief firmly into the lower half of a drinking glass. Be sure that the handkerchief will not fall out when the glass is turned upside down. Fill a large pot or a sink with water. Push the glass, open end down, below the surface of the water. The handkerchief will remain dry because the air in the glass occupies space and therefore prevents the water from rising into the glass.

THE MOVING APPLES

Suspend two apples so that they hang about half an inch apart. When they hang absolutely still, place your mouth close to the space between the apples and blow hard. Instead of flying apart, the apples will move closer together. Whenever air moves fast, its pressure is lowered. With the pressure between the apples lessened, the normal air pressure on the rest of the apples' surfaces pushes them together.

THE SPINNING SPIRAL

Cut a spiral out of a piece of paper. Balance your spiral on the point of a pencil. To do this, you may have to press the paper down lightly upon the pencil point, but do not press hard enough to make a hole in the paper. Hold the spiral over a lighted electric bulb or over the shade of a lighted lamp. Your spiral will spin around the pencil because the rising warm air pushes the spiral around.

THE FALLING PAPER

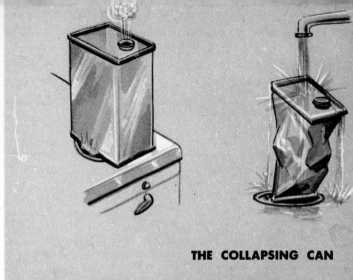

THE COLLAPSING CAN

THE FLOATING EGG

THE SWIMMING FISH

THE FALLING PAPER

Crumple a sheet of paper tightly into a wad. Hold the paper wad and a flat sheet of paper at the same height above your head. Hold the sheet parallel to the floor. Let go of both pieces of paper at the same moment. The paper wad will strike the floor before the sheet. The rounded surface of the paper wad offers less resistance to the air than the flat paper sheet. Streamlined airplanes, automobiles, and trains have rounded surfaces so as to offer less resistance to the air they move through.

THE COLLAPSING CAN

Obtain a gallon can with a screw-cap that fits tightly. Pour a glass of water into the can. Heat the can on a gas range until steam pours from the opening. Turn off the heat. Using a potholder, quickly place the can in the sink and screw the cap on tightly. Run cold water over the can. The can will buckle and collapse. The steam drove the air out of the can, and when, in the cooled can, the steam condensed to water, a partial vacuum was formed. As a result, the greater air pressure on the outside crushed the can.

THE FLOATING EGG

Place an egg into a tall glass of water, and watch it sink to the bottom. Add a tablespoon of salt to the water and carefully stir it until the salt dissolves. By the time you have finished this operation, the egg will be floating at the surface of the water. (If not, add more salt.) A volume of salt water equal to the volume of the egg weighs more than the egg and therefore pushes the egg to the surface.

THE SWIMMING FISH

Cut a piece of cardboard or stiff paper into the shape of a fish. Cut into the tail of the fish a channel that ends in a hole about one-eighth of an inch in diameter. Suspend a drop of oil in this hole. Place the fish on the surface of a panful of water. The fish will move forward under its own power because the oil lessens the surface tension behind the fish. (You can use a piece of soap or camphor in place of the oil.)

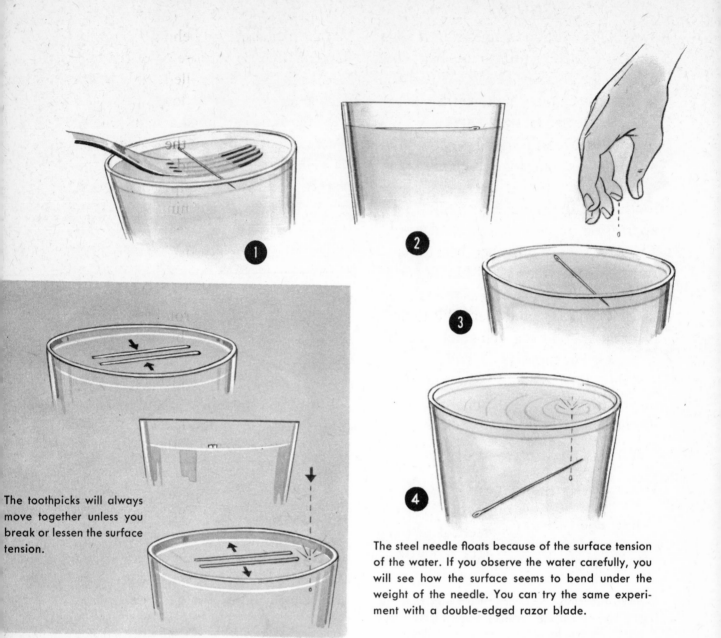

The toothpicks will always move together unless you break or lessen the surface tension.

The steel needle floats because of the surface tension of the water. If you observe the water carefully, you will see how the surface seems to bend under the weight of the needle. You can try the same experiment with a double-edged razor blade.

Everyone knows that steel will not float.

How can you make steel float? Steel is nearly eight times as heavy as water. Yet it is easy to make a piece of steel float. Place a sewing needle upon the tines of a fork. Lower the fork into a glass filled with water. The needle will float. The needle is made of steel. Why does it float?

Water is made up of tiny particles called *molecules*. The molecules attract each other like tiny magnets. The mole-

cules at the surface of a liquid attract each other strongly enough to be able to support small weights, such as a needle. This molecular attraction at the surface of liquids is called *surface tension*.

When you have floated the needle, obtain some soap powder or detergent powder. Soap and detergent clean because they lessen the surface tension of water, and cause oils and greases to form tiny particles that can be washed away. Drop just one single grain of soap powder or detergent into the glass containing the floating needle. Watch the needle immediately sink, as the surface tension is lessened.

The surface of a liquid is actually in a state of tension; that is, it exists as if it were being pulled tight. Place two toothpicks about one-eighth of an inch apart, side by side, in a glass of water. They will move together because the surface of the water is a little higher at the sides of the glass. It is as though you placed two iron pipes near the middle of a blanket that was being held taut by its edges. The pipes would roll together.

Add a few grains of soap powder or detergent to the water, and watch the toothpicks fly apart, as the surface tension is lessened.

How does water help to generate electricity?

Water is a fairly heavy substance. You will prove this for yourself, if you try to lift a bucket filled with water. Water falling long distances can perform much work. Water is put to work

by first penning it up behind a dam. In the dam are one or more openings that lead to a long pipe called a *penstock*. The penstock curves downward — in some dams, for as much as half a mile. Water from behind the dam falls through the penstock and comes out the bottom of this long pipe with great force. At the lower opening of the penstock is a *turbine*, a great wheel with blades radiating outward from its center. Water shooting out of the penstock strikes the blades of the turbine, and spins the great wheel around very rapidly. The axle of the turbine runs to an electric generator, which it turns. In this way, water generates electricity.

Push a knitting needle through the exact center of a cork. Stick half a dozen pens into the outside of the cork, in a

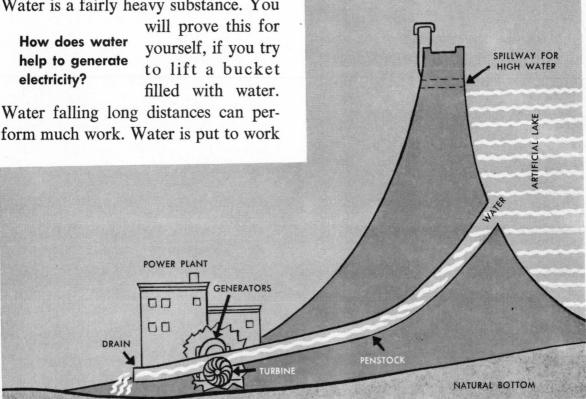

Water is put to work to help create electricity.

23

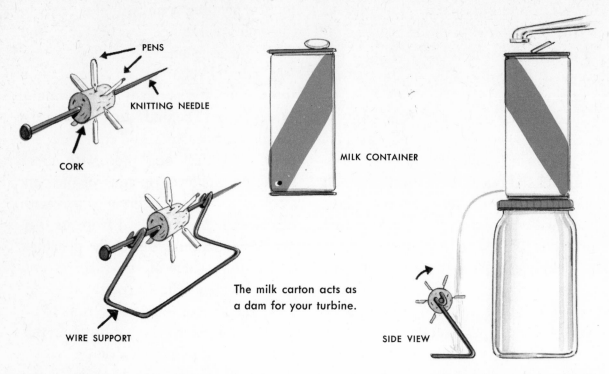

PENS

KNITTING NEEDLE

CORK

MILK CONTAINER

The milk carton acts as a dam for your turbine.

WIRE SUPPORT

SIDE VIEW

circle. Twist a coat hanger into the shape shown in the illustration. Place the knitting needle on the wire cradle as shown. This is your turbine. Punch a small hole near the bottom of a milk carton. Place the carton beneath a faucet in a sink, and arrange the turbine so that water running out of the hole in the carton strikes the pens. Your turbine will spin rapidly, as long as water continues to shoot out of the carton, which is acting as the dam.

How does water rise to the tops of trees?

In the Sequoia National Park in California, some of the trees are thirty stories tall. Water rises from their roots to their tops. How does this take place? Put a few drops of red, or green, or blue ink into a glassful of water. Put a piece of uncooked macaroni into the water vertically. Note that the water inside the macaroni rises higher than the surface of the water outside. The reason for the

The water inside the macaroni rises higher than the surface of the water outside.

Capillary action makes the water rise from the roots of plants to the highest leaves.

24

rise of water inside the tube of macaroni is that the water molecules are attracted to the sides of the tube, and "creep" up the sides. The rise of liquids in thin tubes is called *capillary action*. The thinner the tube, the higher the rise.

Inside all woody plants there are thousands of tubes. So small is the diameter of each tube that it is hard to see it with the naked eye. It is capillary action in these tubes that raises water to the tops of plants, including the tallest trees.

Put a freshly-cut celery stalk into colored water. After a few hours, note that the leaves are colored by the water that has risen through the stalk by capillary action.

Sound

What is sound?

The world is full of sound. In the streets of a busy town, we hear the honking of auto horns, the rumble of trucks, the screech of brakes, shouts, thumps, clangs, and dozens of other sounds you can easily name. Indoor sounds are familiar to all: footsteps on the floor, the thud of closing doors, people talking, music and voice from television or radio, the rattle of dishes, silverware, and kitchen utensils. In the country, you may hear the songs of birds, cawing of crows, lowing of cattle, the buzz-

ing of insects, or the rustle of leaves as a breeze blows through the trees. Even in the quietest night, you can hear your own breathing. There is no time when you are awake that you cannot hear sounds.

When an object vibrates — moves rapidly back and forth — sound is produced.

A vibrating object produces sound.

Obtain a ruler or a wooden lath. Place it on a table, so that about two-thirds of the ruler projects over the edge of the table. Hold the ruler firmly with the palm of one hand. Pull the free end of the ruler down about an inch, and then suddenly let go. Do you see the ruler vibrate at the same time you hear the deep hum it makes? When it stops vibrating, place your ear close to the ruler. Now, you hear no sound coming from the ruler. Clearly then, the vibration of the ruler had something to do with the sound it made.

Hold a dinner fork close to your ear, and listen carefully. No sound comes from the fork. Strike the edge of the fork against a table or some other hard object. Note the prongs' blurry appearance caused by their rapid vibration. Again, strike the fork against the table, and quickly bring the fork close to your ear. You will easily hear the sound coming from the rapidly-moving prongs. So,

25

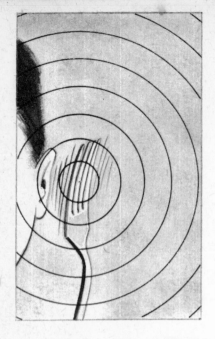

No sound will come from the tines of a dinner fork unless you make the prongs vibrate.

again, we have connected vibration and sound.

How does sound travel? You surely know that sound always travels from the source of the sound. A friend shouts to you, and you know that the sound of his voice travels from his throat to your ears. You hear the sound of an airplane's engine because sound travels from the engine to you. You probably can name a hundred instances in your daily experience in which sound travels from its source to your ears. Even the sound of your own voice has to travel from your vocal cords to your ears.

Can we perform an experiment that will show us something about how sound travels? We can, if we use a bell jar. The bell jar rests, open side down, on a circular metal plate that has a hole in its center. A rubber tube runs from this hole to a pump that can pull air out of the bell jar.

We set an alarm clock to go off in one minute, and place the clock on a sponge on the metal plate. We coat the rim of the bell jar with grease, such as petroleum jelly, before placing it on the metal plate. The grease prevents air from leaking in or out of the bell jar. Soon, we clearly hear the clock ring.

We remove the bell jar, wind the alarm, set it to go off in five minutes, and replace the clock, sponge, and bell jar on the metal plate. Now, we start the pump pulling air out of the bell jar. When, at the end of five minutes, the alarm rings, we can barely hear it. What has happened? We guess that lack of air in the bell jar has diminished the amount of sound that the alarm produces. Our guess is right. If all the air were pumped out of the bell jar, we would not hear the alarm at all — because the alarm would make no sound whatever. From this experiment we can

conclude that air was needed for the vibrations of the alarm to travel in the form of sound. The air is called the *medium* in which the sound traveled. The word "medium" comes from the Latin word *medius,* which means "middle." The air served as a middle, or go-between, that conducted the vibrations from the bell to your ear, so that you heard them as sound.

We know that air is quite a satisfactory medium for the travel of sound, because, except when we are swimming or in the bathtub, sounds always reach our ears through air. Air is a mixture of several gases, so we can say that gases are a

What is the best medium for sound to travel through?

satisfactory medium for sound. Liquids are a better medium than gases; and solids are even better than liquids.

Next time you are swimming, try this experiment. Ask a friend to stand about fifty feet from you and to strike two medium-sized rocks together. Put your head under water, and ask your friend

Water is better than air as a conductor of sound.

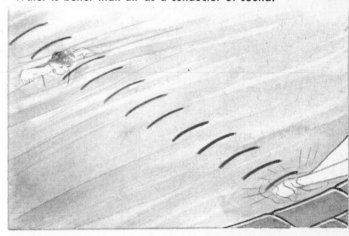

to strike the rocks together, again, this time beneath the surface of the water. You will notice that the sound of the striking rocks is louder under water. This shows that water is better than air as a medium for carrying sound.

To learn how well solids conduct

A bell jar is expensive. For home experimentation, use instead a large peanut butter jar.

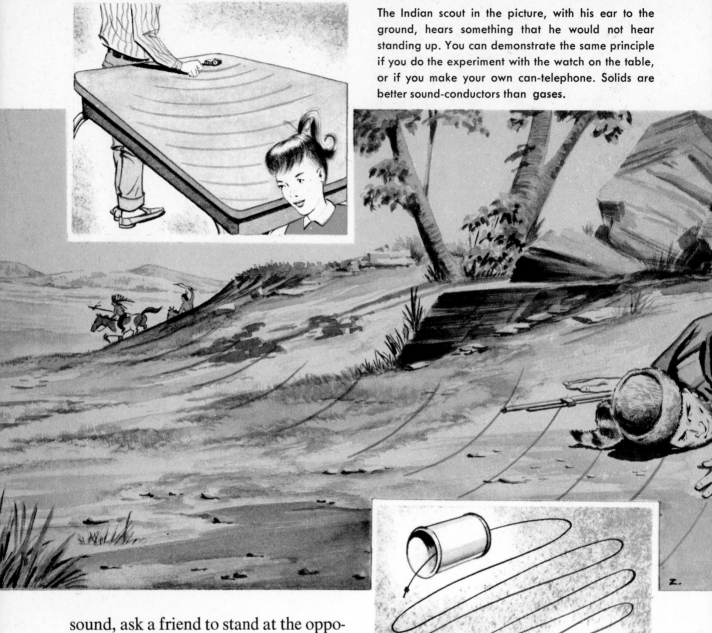

The Indian scout in the picture, with his ear to the ground, hears something that he would not hear standing up. You can demonstrate the same principle if you do the experiment with the watch on the table, or if you make your own can-telephone. Solids are better sound-conductors than gases.

sound, ask a friend to stand at the opposite end of a bare table with a watch in his hand. You will hardly hear the ticking of the watch, if you hear it at all. Now, have your friend place the watch on his end of the table while you put an ear to the top of your end of the table. You will hear the watch ticking quite clearly. This shows that the table which is solid, is a better sound-conducting medium than air, which is gas.

Another experiment that shows that solids conduct sound better than gases is this: Thread a length of stout string,

about thirty feet long, through a hole in the bottom of each of two empty tin cans. Now, tie thick knots at the ends of the string so that they will not slip back through the holes. Ask a friend to take one of the cans and walk away from you until the string is taut. Ask him to speak in a very low voice, so that you can barely hear him. Then ask him to speak in the same level of voice into his tin can, while you hold yours to your ear. Now, you will hear his voice more loudly, for the string conducts sound better than air does.

We have learned that sound must have

What are sound waves? a medium in which to travel. We still have to learn in what form sound travels through the medium. The vibrating prongs of a tuning fork produce sound. Let us concentrate on the action of one prong. As the prong moves in one direction, it compresses the air particles in front of it. Then, the prong swings in the opposite direction, and the space that it just occupied is nearly empty of air particles. The surrounding air particles begin to crowd into the partly-empty space, but the prong, swinging forward again, compresses them once more. This process of compressing and rarefying the air around the prong continues as long as the prong vibrates.

The compressed particles of air are pushed against those a little farther away from the prong. This push, or *impulse,* moves farther and farther outward, compressing air particles as it travels. Following behind the compression is a space of rarefied air. Thus, the vibrating prong sends through the air a continual series of alternating compressions and rarefactions. Each pair of compressions and rarefactions makes up one *sound wave.* Sound waves travel outward from a vibrating object like a series of expanding soap bubbles, each one inside the one moving ahead of it.

Scientists have very fast cameras with which they can photograph sound waves. We do not have such a camera, but we can perform experiments that will give us an idea of how sound waves travel.

Run four or five inches of water into a bathtub, washbowl, or kitchen sink. You will need a light above the water, and the ceiling light will do very well.

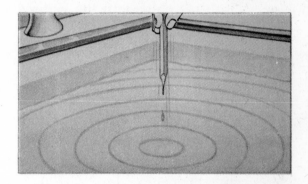

Sharply tap the center of the water with a pencil. Do you see, on the bottom, shadows of a series of rings moving outward from the place where you tapped the water? The rings are crests of water waves.

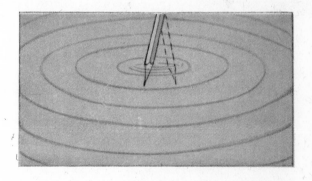

Now dip the pencil into the center of the water. Wag the pencil back and forth rapidly; that is, make the pencil vibrate. You again produce a series of expanding circular water waves that move outward from the pencil, each circle inside the one moving ahead of it. The shadows of the waves are what

29

you would see if you could slice a series of sound waves in half and then look at the cut edges.

It is important to understand that sound waves are not made up of particles of air that move outward from the vibrating object. It is only the push, or impulse, that moves.

From a piece of wood shave half a dozen chips no more than half an inch long. Drop the chips into the water in several locations. Use the pencil to produce more water waves, and note that although the chips may move about a bit, their main motion is to bob up and down as the waves pass them by. If the waves had been made up of water moving outward from the pencil, they would have carried the chips along with them; but they did not. This fact shows us that water waves are simply up-and-down motions that travel along the surface of the water. Knowing this helps us to understand that sound waves are simply pushes that compress and rarefy the air as they travel outward from a vibrating object.

Another experiment that will help you to understand the idea of a moving impulse is the following. Place six coins in a straight row on a smooth table top. Place a seventh coin a half inch behind the row. With a flip of your finger against the seventh coin, cause it to slide along the table and strike the coin at the rear of the row. You will see that the front coin suddenly moves forward away from the row. What moved the front coin? The push you gave the seventh coin traveled all along the row and moved the front coin forward. The other coins remained in place. In much the same way, particles of air remain in place as the push, or impulse, of a sound wave moves through them.

What is an echo?

Once again, sharply tap the center of the water. Observe the wave shadows carefully. Note that when they reach the sides of the container, they bounce back

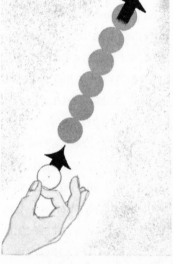

If you imagine the coins to be particles of air, you can demonstrate how they remain in place as the impulse of a sound wave moves through them.

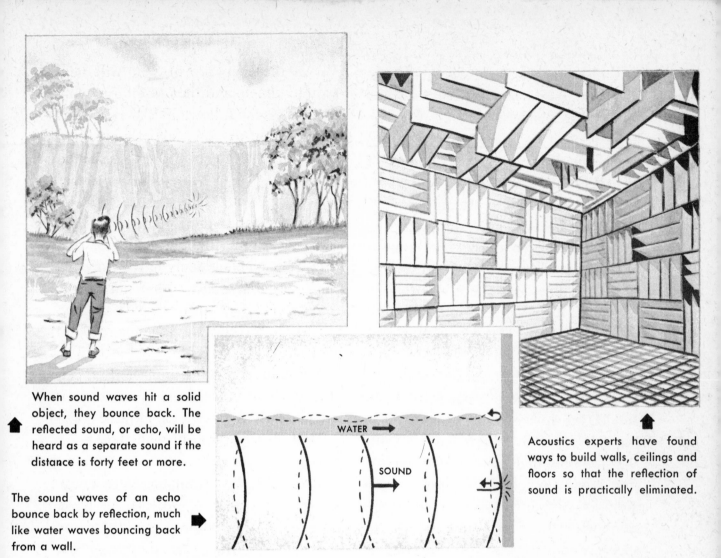

When sound waves hit a solid object, they bounce back. The reflected sound, or echo, will be heard as a separate sound if the distance is forty feet or more.

The sound waves of an echo bounce back by reflection, much like water waves bouncing back from a wall.

WATER

SOUND

Acoustics experts have found ways to build walls, ceilings and floors so that the reflection of sound is practically eliminated.

toward the center. When waves bounce in this manner, they are said to be *reflected*. You are familiar with the reflection of light. The reflection of sound waves from objects they strike is almost exactly the same as the reflection of light from shiny objects. A reflected sound is an *echo*.

If you are in the country, and if you shout your name toward a steep grassy hill or toward the foot of a cliff, the sound of your voice will travel to the hill or cliff and then reflect back as an echo, as though someone in front of you were calling you.

If you shout toward a thickly wooded hill, you will probably hear no echo at all, or only a faint one. The reason for

this is that the sound of your voice will strike the leaves, twigs, and branches of the trees. As a result, the sound waves will be reflected at the hundreds of different angles toward which the surfaces of the leaves, twigs, and branches are facing. Only a few surfaces will reflect sound back to you, and usually these are too few to produce an echo loud enough to be heard.

It is interesting to know that sound engineers who want to diminish echoes in theaters copy the manner in which the trees on the wooded hill diminished the echo of your voice. The engineers may build the walls and ceiling of the theater with rippled surfaces, so that sound is reflected at many angles, allow-

31

ing very little sound to echo to the seats or stage or movie screen. Or else, the sound engineers may cover walls and ceiling with materials that have tiny holes in their surfaces. Sound bounces around in the holes, unable to echo from the walls and ceiling.

If you live in a city, finding a place to hear echoes may be difficult. You must find a large open space that is shielded from traffic and other city noises. At one end of this open space must be a high wall or some other flat surface. An empty lot with a billboard at one end makes an excellent echoing place. Since the distance at which you can stand from the billboard will probably be much shorter than the distance you can stand away from a hill, you will probably find that the first part of your name has echoed back to you before you finish shouting your whole name. For this reason you will probably have difficulty hearing any echo at all. To remedy this situation, shout a short syllable, such as *ba,* or else clap your hands. These sounds will echo clearly.

Sound travels approximately 1,100 feet

How can you measure distance with sound?

per second in air that has a temperature of 70° Fahrenheit. We can use this fact to measure distance. Thunder is sound echoing from cloud to cloud and from cloud to earth. The source of thunder is a lightning flash — a giant electric spark that suddenly and intensely heats the air through which it passes. The heated air expands so rapidly that it gives the neighboring air a powerful push. This push travels as a

The number of seconds between lightning and thunder divided by five will give you the distance in miles from the lightning flash to you.

great sound wave that we hear — if we are close to the lightning — as a thunderclap. If we are far from the lightning, we hear the familiar rumbling of thunder, as the thunderclap echoes from clouds and hills.

With these facts in mind, we are ready to use sound to measure distance. We have to wait for a thunderstorm, and we need a watch with a second hand. When we see a flash of lightning, we note the exact time according to the second hand of the watch. Light travels so fast — 186,000 miles per second — that we can ignore the time it takes light to travel from the lightning flash to our watch. Having timed the moment at which the lightning flashed, we keep our eyes on the watch's second hand to learn how many seconds it will take the first sound of thunder to reach our ears. Since we know that sound travels approximately 1,100 feet per second, we multiply by 1,100 the number of seconds between the lightning flash and the first sound of thunder. This gives the distance in feet from us to the lightning flash. Suppose it took five seconds for the sound of thunder to reach us. We multiply 5 by 1,100 and obtain 5,500, the number of feet from us to the lightning flash. Since 1,100 feet are roughly one-fifth of a mile, we may find the distance of the lightning in miles by dividing the number of seconds by 5. Using the five seconds in the foregoing example, we divide them by 5, and the result is 1; that is, one mile. Since there are 5,280 feet in a mile, and since we found the lightning to be 5,500 feet distant, we can see that our measurement of distance by means of sound was fairly accurate.

Guitar, banjo, and zither strings are

How do stringed instruments produce sound?

plucked with the fingers or a pick. Violin and cello strings are stroked with a bow. Piano strings are struck with felt hammers. In whatever manner they are played, the strings are caused to vibrate, and thereby to produce sound. But you know that stringed instruments can produce a great variety of sound. Let us see how they vary their sounds.

Fasten shut the lid of a cigar box by gluing it or by nailing it with thin tacks or brads. Drill or cut six holes in the top of the box. In both these operations, be careful not to split the wood.

Break half a dozen rubber bands, so that you can pull them out into single lengths. Use thumbtacks to fasten one end of each rubber band to one end of the top of the box. Fasten the other end of each rubber band to the other end of the box. If the rubber bands are longer than the top of the box, just make sure that the length of each rubber band between thumbtacks is pulled tight. Space the rubber bands evenly apart. Try to get rubber bands of several different thicknesses, and arrange them in order from thickest to thinnest.

Cut two pieces of cardboard that are two inches wide and three inches long. Then draw three lines half an inch apart down the length of each piece of cardboard, thus dividing it into four half-inch strips. Fold each piece of cardboard along its lines so as to make a triangular strip, as shown in the illustration on this page. Fasten the cardboard triangles with adhesive tape. Slip the triangles under the rubber bands, about an inch from each end of the cigar box. Now you have a stringed musical instrument on which you can play tunes by plucking the rubber bands.

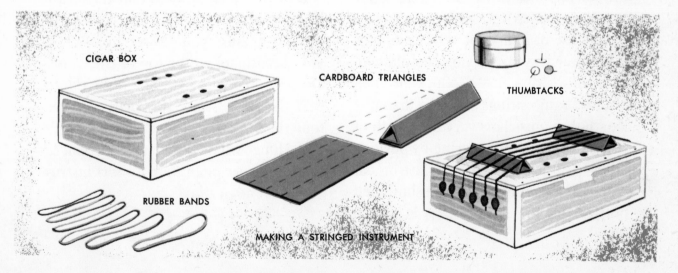

CIGAR BOX
CARDBOARD TRIANGLES
THUMBTACKS
RUBBER BANDS
MAKING A STRINGED INSTRUMENT

As you pluck the rubber bands, note that the thicker ones produce tones of lower pitch than the thin ones. Thick strings on musical instruments are used to produce lower tones, and thin strings to produce higher tones.

Remove the rubber bands from your musical carton, and replace them with six other rubber bands, all of the same thickness. From what we have just learned about the thickness of a musical string and its pitch, we should not be surprised to find that all the strings of our musical carton now have the same pitch. Pluck them and listen. Now, move one of the cardboard triangles, so that it slants across the carton. The result of this move will be to change the

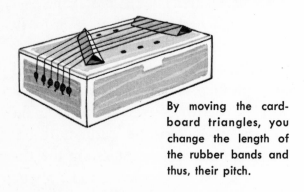

By moving the cardboard triangles, you change the length of the rubber bands and thus, their pitch.

length of those parts of the rubber bands that are between the two triangles. Pluck the rubber bands, and note that the longer ones have low pitch, while the shorter ones have high pitch.

The use of strings of various lengths is another way of varying the pitch of stringed instruments. Violin, cello, guitar, and banjo strings are all of the same length, but musicians vary the length of the vibrating part of a string by pushing it against the neck of the instrument with a finger. Sound from the shortened portion of the string rises in pitch.

Pianos, harps, and harpsichords have strings of different lengths.

Push the triangular piece of cardboard back to its original position. Grasp one of the rubber bands and pull it tighter than its neighbor. Pluck these two rubber bands, one at a time. Note that the tighter one has the higher pitch. Thus, we have a third way in which the pitch of stringed instruments can be varied — by tightening and loosening the strings. You probably have seen a violinist or guitarist tuning his instrument by turning pegs, or keys, at the end of the instrument's neck. In this way, he tightens and loosens strings.

How do wind instruments produce sound?

Flutes, piccolos, tubas, saxophones, clarinets, and trombones are among the many wind instruments. When a musician blows into a wind instrument, he causes a column of air inside the instrument to vibrate, and the vibration produces sound waves. A wide wind instrument produces lower tones than a narrow one. A tuba produces lower notes than a flute.

Obtain a wide drinking straw and a narrow one. Place your finger over one end of the thick straw. Hold the straw in a vertical position, its open end pressed against your lower lip. Below your breath across the top of the straw. Do the same with the thin straw. Note that the thick straw produces a lower tone than the thin straw.

A long wind instrument produces tones of lower pitch than a short instru-

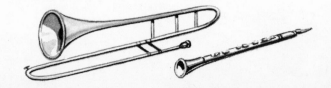

ment. A trombone produces lower notes than a piccolo.

Fill a soda bottle three-quarters full of water. Place a drinking straw in the water. Hold the straw in your right hand and the bottle in your left. Blow across the top of the straw to produce a sound.

The thick straw produces a lower tone than the thin straw.

THE "WATER TROMBONE"

DRINKING GLASS XYLOPHONE

DO RE MI FA SO LA TI DO

Lower the bottle with your left hand, while continuing to blow across the straw. Note that as you lower the bottle, and thereby lengthen the column of air in the straw, the note you are producing lowers in pitch. This is the principle on which the slide trombone works.

Drums, cymbals, xylophones, and vibra-

How do percussion instruments produce sound?

phones are percussion instruments. Upon being struck a blow, some part of a percussion instrument vibrates and thereby produces sound. When you strike a drumhead, it vibrates and sets the air inside the drum to vibrating; this magnifies the sound produced. A struck cymbal is simply a vibrating disc of brass. Different tones of a xylophone are produced by pieces of hardwood of different lengths and thicknesses set vibrating by blows of a small wooden mallet.

Set eight drinking glasses, all of the same size, in a row. Pour half an inch of water into the first glass. Into each succeeding glass pour a little more water than in the glass before it, so that the eighth glass is about three-quarters full. Tap the rim of each glass with a pencil. The differences in the lengths of the air columns in the glasses give them different pitches. Your row of glasses is a sort of xylophone on which you can play tunes.

GALILEO'S
TELESCOPE

Astronomy

NORTH STAR

LITTLE DIPPER

BIG DIPPER

What is astronomy? The word *astronomy* comes from two ancient Greek words that mean "to arrange stars." Ancient Greek astronomers made maps of the night sky, and in doing so, they arranged the stars into groups called *constellations*. The Greeks' study of the stars led to the discovery of many facts about other heavenly bodies — the planets, the sun, and the moon. The ancient Greeks had no telescopes, yet they did a remarkable job of describing heavenly bodies. They mapped more than one-third of the constellations we know today, and they described orbits of five of the planets. Other ancient "star-arrangers," or *astronomers,* carried on the work of mapping stars, so that by the second century A.D., the great Egyptian astronomer Ptolemy had mapped more than half the constellations. By that time, he had also worked out a very ingenious system of circular paths to account for the motion of the planets and the apparent motion of the stars.

Astronomy took a giant step forward when the Dutch optician Hans Lippershey, in 1608 invented the telescope, and the Italian scientist Galileo made the first really effective telescope the following year.

Today, astronomers have huge telescopes and space-piercing cameras with which to study the sun, moon, planets, and stars in the vast spaces of the universe. Let us perform some astronomical experiments.

How can you locate the North Star? For more than a thousand years, mariners in the Northern Hemisphere have been guiding their ships by a bright star that is almost exactly in line with the North Pole. This star is called the North Star, the Pole Star, or Polaris. Of course, with the invention of the compass, mariners found less need for the star that enabled them to tell which direction was north. Modern radio-direction-finding has almost eliminated the need for the North Star. But, since this star played so important a part in navigation for so many hundreds of years, let us see whether we can locate it.

On a clear, cloudless night, when the moon is not up, go outdoors and wait a few minutes for your eyes to become

The Egyptian pyramids, monumental burial tombs of ancient rulers, were also used as points by which stars could be sighted.

Dubhe and Merak, two stars in the Big Dipper, are used to locate the North Star. Regardless of the season of the year, or the location of other stars in the Big Dipper, the Pointer stars always point to the North Star. (See the illustration below.)

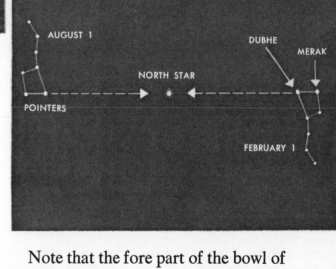

adjusted to the darkness. You must find a location where lighted advertising signs and street lights will not interfere with your seeing.

Look toward the north until you see a group of seven stars that look like points along a dipper with a curved handle. When you have found such a group, or constellation, look around in the same direction for another constellation. It is also in the shape of a dipper, but with the handle curving in the opposite manner from that of the first dipper. The larger of these two is the Big Dipper, and the other is the Little Dipper. They are sometimes called Ursa Major (Big Bear) and Ursa Minor (Little Bear). However, some astronomers consider the Dippers as only parts of Ursa Major and Minor.

Note that the fore part of the bowl of the Big Dipper is made up of two stars. The one at the top of the bowl is called Dubhe, the bottom one, Merak. These two stars are known as the Pointers, because if you draw a line from Merak to Dubhe, and continue the line for a distance equal to about four times the distance between the Pointers, you will arrive at a bright star that is the one we are seeking — the North Star. When you do this, you will probably notice that the North Star is the first star in the handle of the Little Dipper.

No matter what the season of the year, the Pointers always point to the North Star, although, because of the earth's revolution around the sun, the other stars in the Big Dipper seem to shift their positions.

The vast number of stars you see in the sky are all in motion. Some stars are moving thousands of miles per second, but all stars are so far from the earth that they seem to stand still. You can understand this if you think about the fact that a car moving fifty miles per hour seems to whisk rapidly past you, when you are standing by the side of the road; but if you are looking down from a mountain top at a car several miles away and also moving fifty miles per hour, the car now seems to be crawling very slowly. With these facts in mind let us perform our experiment.

How can you use the stars to prove that the earth turns on its axis?

You will need a camera. Any kind of camera will do that has a shutter that can be made to remain open for a time exposure. Load the camera with the most sensitive panchromatic film you can obtain. Your photographic dealer will tell you what kind of film to use.

It is very important now to find a location where there are no interfering lights. A moonless winter night, when the stars are brightest, is best.

Mount your camera on a tripod or some other firm support. Point the camera at the North Star. Try hard to locate the North Star exactly in the center of the camera's finder. Clamp the camera firmly in this position. Set the shutter for a time exposure and click the shutter release. Leave the shutter open for an hour. At the end of this time, be sure to click the shutter release again, to close the shutter.

When the film is developed and a picture is printed from it, you will see many curved white lines against a dark background, and in the center a white spot.

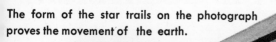
The form of the star trails on the photograph proves the movement of the earth.

If you have successfully centered the North Star, it will be the white spot. The curved lines are the paths of stars. However, we have learned that the stars may be considered as standing still. Therefore, it must have been the camera that turned. But the camera was clamped in one position so that it could not turn. So we are finally led to explain the apparent motion of the stars by saying that it was the earth, upon which the camera was standing, that turned.

Since the camera's shutter was open for one hour, and since we know that the earth makes one complete rotation on its axis in one day — that is, twenty-four hours — we realize that each star path in our picture represents one twenty-fourth of a complete circle.

On a large sheet of paper, draw a circle at least eight inches in **How can you tell the date by the stars?** diameter. Divide the circle into twelve equal parts, just as a clock face is divided. Alongside each division of the circle, write the name of one of the months where an hour num-

ber would be on a clock. Start with March in the 12 position; that is, at the top. Keep the months in their usual order, but write them counterclockwise. Mark the center of the circle "North Star." Imagine that the distance on the circle between each month is divided into thirty smaller divisions.

If you are allowed to stay up until midnight on some clear night, take your diagram outdoors. Hold it so that March is at the top. Imagine the diagram in the sky, with the North Star as the center. Note the location of the Big Dipper. Now draw the Big Dipper on your diagram in the same location as you find it in the sky. When you have done this, draw a straight line from the Pointers to the North Star. This line will pass through the circle at a point that will indicate the date on which you are making your observation. Suppose the line passes halfway between the June and July positions on the circle; then it is June 15. Of course, unless you have

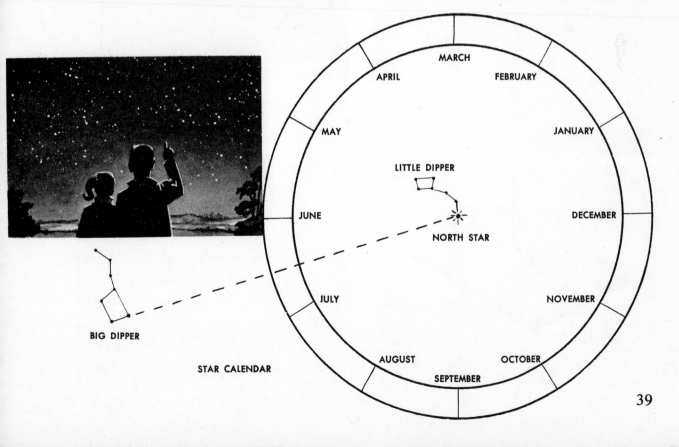

STAR CALENDAR

BIG DIPPER

MARCH
APRIL
FEBRUARY
MAY
JANUARY
LITTLE DIPPER
JUNE
DECEMBER
NORTH STAR
JULY
NOVEMBER
AUGUST
OCTOBER
SEPTEMBER

drawn a very large circle, it will be difficult to estimate thirty divisions between months on the circle. However, you can come within a few days of the exact date. The important thing is to note that on the diagram you have made, on any particular date at midnight, the Pointers are in line with that date on the star calendar.

More than 3,500 years ago, people realized that the sun could be used to tell the time of day. As a result, they learned how to construct instruments called *sundials*. A shadow cast by the sun pointed to the time of day on a dial that was part of a sundial. The Egyptians made great sundials whose pointers were pyramids and obelisks. Perhaps the largest sundial ever built was constructed at Jaipur, India, in 1724. The pointer of this huge sundial is one-hundred feet high, and the whole instrument covers an acre of ground. Some sundials were small enough to be carried about by their owners. For more than a century after watches and

How can you tell time by the sun?

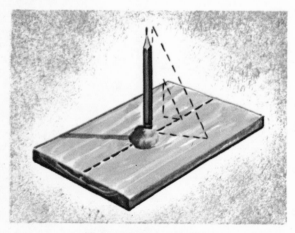

Make your own sundial.

clocks were in use, their accuracy was checked by sundials.

Draw a straight line through the middle of a board and parallel to one side. In the middle of this line, place a gob of modeling clay. Push the blunt end of a pencil down into the clay, so that the pencil stands upright. Be sure that the pencil is perpendicular to the board; to do this, use a carpenter's square or some other square edge. You have made a sundial.

On a sunny morning, set the sundial

in direct sunlight, with the line on the board running from north to south. You will probably need a magnetic compass to accomplish this positioning. Exactly on each hour, as timed by a watch or clock, make a mark on the board at the exact location of the shadow of the pencil point. Write the hour above the mark. Do not move the board at all.

Leave the board in position. On the next sunny day, you will find that the shadow of the pencil will point to the correct time of day. Leave the board in position for a month or two. Or else, make marks on whatever the board was standing, exactly at the ends of the north-south line on the board. Then, at the end of a month or two, you will be able to replace the board in the exact position in which it was originally.

Having come back to your sundial after a month or two, you will see that it no longer is accurate. Why? As the earth circles around the sun, the sun seems to change the path it makes across the sky. (Of course, the sun is not really moving; the earth's motion makes the sun seem to move.) As the path of the sun changes, so does the accuracy of your sundial, because you made the sundial by means of the sun's path on a particular date. The sundial seemed to be accurate for a few days because the sun changes its path slowly, and you could not immediately note the change.

Obtain a board eight inches square; that is, the board must have each side exactly eight inches long. Draw two diagonals on the board. Where the lines cross is the center of the board. Using a drawing compass, draw a seven-inch circle whose center is the center of the board. Divide half the circle into twelve equal divisions, and, proceeding clockwise, mark them: 6, 7, 8, 9, 10, 11, 12, 1, 2, 3, 4, 5. You have made the dial.

How can you make a more accurate sundial?

You now have to make the part of the sundial that casts the shadow. This is called the *gnomon* (NO-mon), which is Greek for "the one that knows." On a piece of wood half an inch thick, draw a triangle that has a base three inches long: thus place a protractor at one end of the base, and mark off an angle equal to your latitude. You can find the latitude of the place in which you live by referring to an atlas. Suppose you live in Chicago, which is at a latitude of 42°; then you mark off an angle of 42°. From the end of the base and through the 42° mark, draw a line eight inches long. From the upper end of this line, draw a straight line to the base to complete the triangle. Now, saw this triangle out of the piece of wood.

Draw a line from the center of the dial to the number 12. Make a mark on this line, half an inch from the center. Place the slanted end of the gnomon on this mark, and the rest of the gnomon's base along the line. Using thin nails, so as not to split the wood, nail the gnomon in place. If you wish, you can glue it in place, but if you are going to use the sundial in a location where it

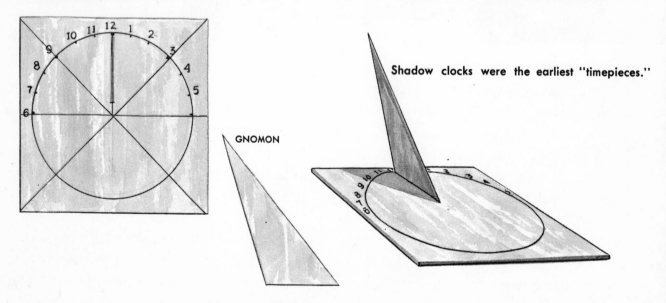

GNOMON

Shadow clocks were the earliest "timepieces."

How you can make a shadow clock.

will be rained upon, it is better to nail down the gnomon. Your sundial is now completed.

Oddly, the best time to set up your sundial is at night. The gnomon must point north. Put the sundial where you want it to remain. Sight along the slant of the gnomon in order to line it up with the North Star. When you have done this, fix the sundial in place, so that it will not easily be moved.

When the sun is shining, you will be able to read the time by noting the number to which the shadow of the gnomon points. But, after all your work, you will be disappointed to find that your sundial is not a very good time-teller. To make your sundial more accurate, you must make an adjustment. On this page is a diagram showing the months and two sets of numbers from 0 to 15. The numbers represent minutes. In the diagram is a curve that is a graph of the *equation of time*. You use the diagram in this manner: Suppose it is February 15. Place a ruler vertically on the dia-

gram where you estimate the middle of February to be. Mark the point at which the edge of the ruler crosses the curved line. Now, turn the ruler horizontally, so that its edge touches the point you have just marked on the curved line. Looking to the left you will see that the ruler cuts the left-hand line at a point about fourteen minutes above the middle horizontal line. Now, read the time on your sundial, and add fourteen minutes to your reading. This is the correct time. The rule for the use of the diagram representing the equation of time is this: For readings above the middle horizontal line, add minutes to the sundial reading; for readings below the middle line, subtract minutes from the sundial reading.

Your sundial does not yet agree with your watch. Don't be disappointed; your sundial is correct, and your watch is wrong. Here is why: as the earth turns, each meridian (a line running from the North to the South Pole) is at a different time. For this reason, prior to

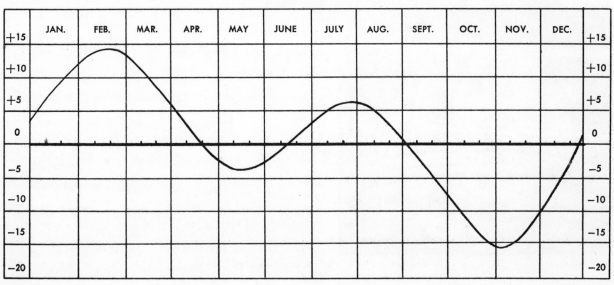

THE EQUATION OF TIME — For readings above center line, add minutes to sundial time; for readings below center line, subtract minutes from sundial time.

about one hundred years ago, each town had time different from that of nearby towns to the east and west. The confusion caused by this situation was ended by deciding on standard time zones. All the places within a standard time zone use the same time; that is, all watches and clocks are set to the same time. In the continental United States, there are Eastern, Central, Mountain, and Pacific standard time zones. The time is an hour earlier in each succeeding zone, going from east to west. So, if it is six o'clock in New York, which is in the Eastern Standard Zone, it is three o'clock in San Francisco, which is in the Pacific Standard Zone. The time shown by your sundial is sun time, or solar time, and (adjusted by the equation of time) is the correct time for the place where your sundial is located. If you live where solar time and standard time coincide, your sundial and your watch will both be right.

Our sun is a star, a medium-sized star,

How can you see sunspots? and like the billions of other stars in the universe, the sun is a great globe of hot, glowing gas. The

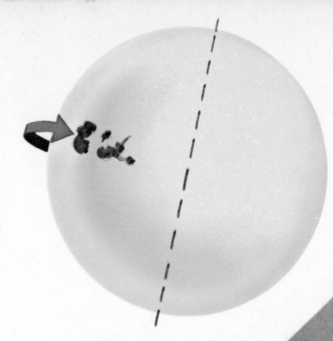

sun is 865,380 miles in diameter, a distance equal to 109 earths in a row. More than 1,000,000 earths would fit into the sun. The temperature at the surface of the sun is 11,000° Fahrenheit, and at the sun's center, the temperature is about 40,000,000° F. The sun is 93,000,000 miles from the earth and the nearly-empty space between has a temperature of 459° F. below zero.

When looking at the sun, we see only its outer surface. This surface is made up of four layers of gas, but we are interested only in the innermost of these layers, the *photosphere*. It is in this layer that sunspots appear. When seen through a large telescope, sunspots look like large, ragged, black holes with a bright border. Astronomers are not at all clear about what causes sunspots or just what they are. Small sunspots are a few thousand miles in diameter, while large ones may be from 50,000 to 150,000 miles across. Several dozen earths could be tossed into the larger sunspots.

Sunspots usually appear in pairs or clusters. They last for a few days, and then disappear. Some spots may last for more than twenty-five days. Most

PALOMAR OBSERVATORY, CALIFORNIA

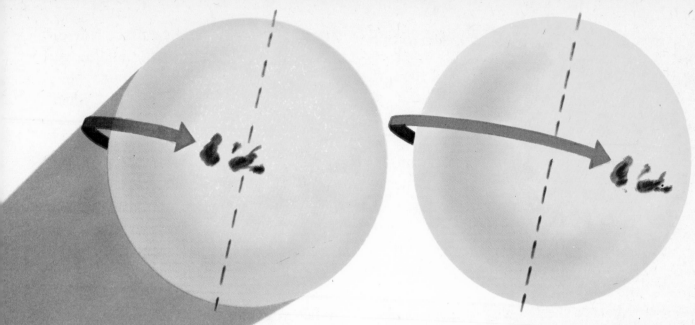

spots are in the middle regions of both the Northern and Southern hemispheres of the sun.

Of course, the best way to see sunspots is by means of a telescope with the proper ray filters that cut out most of the sun's light. (Do not, however, look at the sun through sunglasses; ordinary sunglasses do not cut out enough light. A pair of field glasses without a darkened sun filter should not be used either. Looking directly at the sun without proper protection may cause injury to the eyes.) Lacking the needed ray filter, we can turn to nature to provide one for us. All we have to do is to make our observations at sunrise or sunset on a clear day, when the sun rises or sets red. A red sun tells us that there is a considerable amount of haze in the earth's atmosphere at that particular time, and the haze cuts out enough sunlight so that we can look directly at the sun without hurting our eyes.

Large sunspots can be seen with the naked eye, and medium-sized ones can be seen with a pair of field glasses. By looking through one or two sheets of red cellophane, or by placing the cello-

You can prove rotation of the sun by following the location of the same sunspot on successive days.

EARTH

SUNSPOT

Some sunspots are many times the size of the earth.

phane over the lenses of field glasses, we can lighten the color of the sun and thereby increase the visibility of the dark spots on its surface. If you are watching a rising sun, end your observations when the sun's color becomes orange — as seen by your naked eye, not through the red cellophane. Do not begin to observe the setting sun until it has actually turned red.

There is a way to observe sunspots at any time of day. Stand a pair of binoculars (field glasses) on their front lens casings upon a stout piece of cardboard that is ten inches square. Place the binoculars in the middle of the cardboard, about two inches from the bottom. Run a pencil point around the lens casings, and cut out the two circles you have drawn. Fit the binoculars into the holes you have cut. On a table near a window, place the binoculars and cardboard, so that the binoculars directly face the sun. You may have to use a few books to prop the binoculars in the right position.

Paste a sheet of white paper to a piece of cardboard, in order to stiffen the paper. Focus the binoculars at infinity, or whatever is the focus for seeing farthest. Hold the white paper behind the binoculars, so that the sun's image falls on this white screen. You will probably have to move the screen back and forth — away and toward the binoculars — in order to put the sun in clear focus. When the sun is in focus, you will see sunspots as black dots on the white screen. Don't be discouraged if you do not see any sunspots the first time you

try. Sometimes the sun's surface is free of all but spots that are too small to be seen with binoculars. Continue your observations for several days, and your perseverance will be rewarded.

Keep a daily record of your observations by drawing diagrams of the sun and its spots. Since the sun revolves on its axis, you will see long-lasting sunspots move daily along the sun's surface, and perhaps even disappear around the edge of the sun.

When you have a good sunspot in focus on the white screen behind your binoculars, measure carefully the diameter of the image of the sun and of the sunspot. Suppose your image of the sun is two inches in diameter, and the spot is one-sixteenth of an inch. Then, the spot will have a diameter equal to one-thirty second that of the sun. The diameter of the sun is 865,380 miles, and the diameter of the sunspot is one-thirty second of this distance, or 27,043 miles — a fair-sized spot. Sometimes your observations may not give results so easy to calculate as in the foregoing example. Another way to calculate the sunspot's diameter is this: Multiply the sunspot's image by the diameter of the sun (865,380), and divide your result by the diameter of the sun's image on your screen. The result will be the sunspot's diameter.

How can you measure the size of a sunspot?

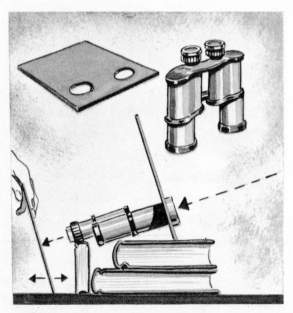

Observe sunspots without looking into the sun.

Perhaps on a clear night you have seen a point of light streak across the sky. You may know that what you saw was a

How can you become a meteor watcher?

Near Winslow, Arizona there is a crater nearly a mile wide. It was made by a meteor that must have exploded into thousands of pieces.

"shooting star," whose scientific name is *meteor*. The space through which the earth is traveling contains a great amount of small objects — pieces of iron and stone. Most of these range in size from that of a grain of dust to that of a grain of rice. A few are much larger. These objects in space are called *meteoroids,* a word that means "resembling meteors." Most meteoroids travel at high speeds; the average speed is twenty-six miles per second. The earth moves around the sun at a speed of eighteen-and-one-half miles per second. When a meteoroid and the earth meet head on, their combined speeds are forty-four-and-one-half miles per second; when a meteoroid catches up to the earth, its speed of collision is twenty-six minus eighteen-and-one-half, or seven-and-one-half miles per second.

When a meteoroid enters the earth's atmosphere, it becomes a meteor. All except the smallest begin to glow brightly at heights of fifty to seventy-five miles, due to the friction caused by their high speed and the resistance of the atmosphere. By the time meteors have plunged to within forty miles of the earth's surface, most of them have burned up, leaving only a momentarily glowing streak of dust behind. Some of the meteors strike the earth's surface, and by doing so become *meteorites.* These vary in size from small grains to those as big as an automobile and weighing many tons. In the Hayden Planetarium in New York City, there is a meteorite, which was found in Greenland, that weighs thirty-six tons. About 100,000,000 meteors bombard the earth every day. They add about 4,000 tons to the weight of the earth per day.

On a clear moonless night, in a location where you have an unobstructed view of the sky and no interfering man-made lights, settle yourself in a comfortable rest, such as a deck chair. Within five to ten minutes, your eyes will become adapted to the dark. To observe meteors properly, you must know directions in the sky. Face the North Star—then behind you is south, to your left is west, and to your right is east. Even better, learn the names of some of the constellations, so that you can locate meteors even more closely than by simply using compass directions. Have with you a pad of paper and pencil, a flashlight covered with red cellophane, and a watch and a ruler.

When you see a meteor, record the hour and minute, and, if possible, the exact second of its appearance. Hold

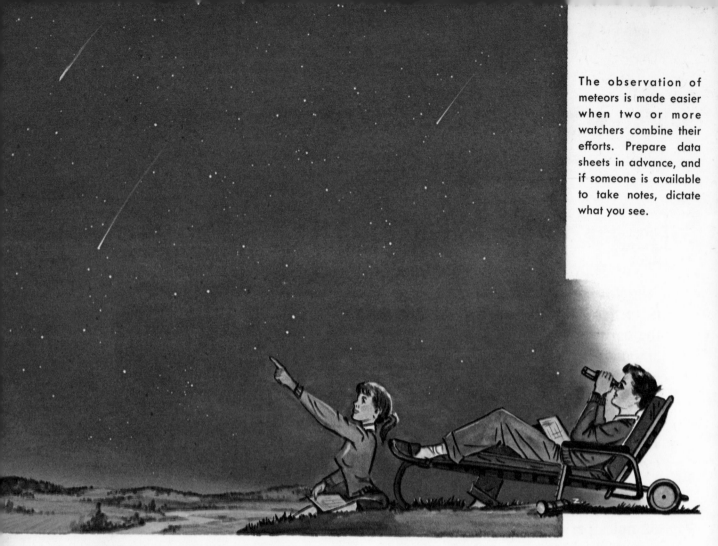

the ruler at arm's length, so that its edge is along the meteor's path. Now, record where the meteor appeared and where it disappeared. Also, record its brightness (very bright, medium, or dim), speed (fast, medium, or slow), how many seconds you think it lasted, and any other comments you wish to make on the meteor's appearance.

If you find this work interesting, you may want to become an official meteor observer. If so, write to the American Meteor Society, 521 North Wynnewood Avenue, Narberth, Pennsylvania. Tell them that you would like to have official report forms and directions for making reports; also, that you would like to obtain sky charts. By reporting to the American Meteor Society, you actually will be participating in the work of astronomers.

On an average night, you may see five to ten meteors an hour. On other nights, when you are experienced enough to spot the faint meteors, you may see forty or fifty. Perhaps you will be as lucky as the observers on the night of November 12, 1833, when 35,000 meteors were observed per hour! Some were as large as the full moon and left trails that lasted fifteen to twenty minutes.

Whether you have performed the experiments in this book or have simply read them, you probably have learned many things about the world around you. And this is always a pleasant experience.

THE HOW AND WHY WONDER BOOK OF
LIGHT AND COLOR

Written by Harold Joseph Highland, B.S., M.S., Ph.D. Associate Professor, Chairman of the Department of Business Administration, College of Business Administration, Long Island University.

Illustrated by George J. Zaffo

Editorial Production: Donald D. Wolf

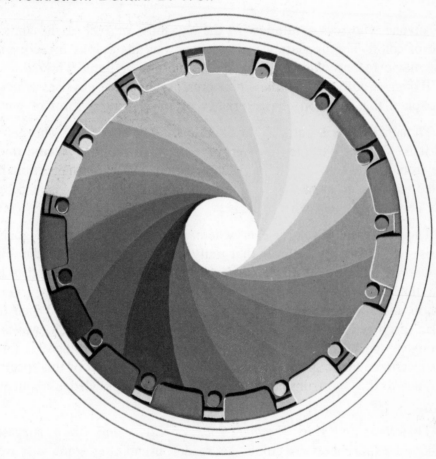

Edited under the supervision of
Dr. Paul E. Blackwood,
Washington, D. C.

Text and illustrations approved by
Oakes A. White, Brooklyn Children's Museum, Brooklyn, N. Y.

GROSSET & DUNLAP • Publishers • NEW YORK

Introduction

Anyone who sees a rainbow in the sky must marvel at the apparent magic of color. The appearance of a rainbow is marvelous indeed, but it is not magic to one who understands the nature of light. This *How and Why Wonder Book of Light and Color* presents the basic physical principles that explain the common characteristics of this essential form of energy.

Though light is a part of our experience day after day, who can say what it is? Is light particles of energy? Is it wave motion? Where does it come from and where does it go? Observation and experimentation have enabled scientists to answer these questions in part, but it is not yet possible to say conclusively just what light is.

There is great diversity everywhere in nature. One of the goals of scientists is to discover patterns that unify our understanding of the apparently unordered universe. In the study of light, for example, scientists have found that heat, X-rays, radio waves and cosmic rays all have a certain common characteristic. They all travel in a wave-like motion. When these rays are arranged according to the length of their waves, radio waves are the longest and cosmic rays are the shortest. This arrangement is known as the electromagnetic spectrum, and light is the visible part of this spectrum. Reference to this spectrum helps scientists organize knowledge about wave energy.

This *How and Why Wonder Book of Light and Color* suggests a number of experiments to guide the reader in making some discoveries about light and color for himself. It is a useful addition to every home or school library where there are potential young scientists at work.

Paul E. Blackwood

Dr. Blackwood is a professional employee in the U. S. Office of Education. This book was edited by him in his private capacity and no official support or endorsement by the Office of Education is intended or should be inferred.

Library of Congress Catalog Card Number: 67-24095

Contents

The Nature of Light

Many many years ago, if we looked in a dictionary, we would find that light was described as the opposite of darkness. **What is light?** Today, scientists tell us that light is a form of energy that radiates or gives off rays just as a pebble creates waves if we dropped it into a pond of water. These rays, or light waves, as they are sometimes called, can travel through space and certain kinds of materials.

Light waves that reach and enter our eyes produce a sensation that we call sight. Light is our guide to the world around us. Because of light we can see our way around our homes; we can see to walk through streets; we can see the sky and we can even read this book. If you closed your eyes, you would not see this page because your eyelids would prevent the light rays from entering your eyes.

Thus, we have established one fact about light: unless the light from an object enters our eyes, we cannot see the object. Some objects, like the sun, stars and the electric bulb give off their own light. They radiate light because they are very hot, or as scientists call them, red-hot and white-hot bodies. The light waves they radiate are known as *incandescent light*. Most of the light we receive is from the largest source of incandescent light — the sun.

Another source of light is produced by electric sparks in tubes containing special gases; that is known as *fluorescent* or *cold light,* and we shall explore this type of light more fully later in this book.

The light we see directly from the source of light, such as the sun, an electric bulb or a fluorescent lamp, is known as *direct light*. If this light is reflected

THE AGES

or bounced off a surface in the same manner as a ball thrown against a wall, the light is known as *indirect* or *reflected light*. The light we see from the moon or the planets is an example of this type of light. It is light from the sun that has been reflected by the surface of the moon or that of the planets before it reaches our eyes.

Light is also a messenger of the universe. The light we see either directly from the sun and stars or indirectly from the moon and planets, tells us not only that they exist, but also enables us to determine their location.

Scientists have told us that light is a form of energy because it produces chemical changes in objects. The light that green plants receive helps the plants to make their food from water and carbon dioxide. We can see that without light, plants would not grow and there would be no food. Another example of chemical change produced by light takes place within every camera. The light striking the specially prepared chemical coating on the film produces

The "direct light" of the sun becomes "indirect light" as it reaches the dark and narrow street after being reflected by a window.

an image or picture on that film. Likewise, the light that strikes the special chemical coating of a photoelectric tube or cell combines with that chemical to produce an electric current.

Furthermore, without the sun's light warming the earth's surface, it would be so terribly cold that life could not exist. Without light, there would be no winds or rain. The winds are created by the sun's heating of the surface of the earth. Some areas of the earth become hotter than others; for example, the sunlight can warm desert sands more than it can the ocean, or warm the fields and city streets more than the icy regions at either the North or South Pole. The difference in temperature between any two heated areas of the earth will cause the air to flow and thus create winds. As the winds move over the earth, they pick up dust and other small particles and these combine with water that has evaporated when the sunlight heated the lakes, ponds, rivers and oceans. The small particles of water and dust form clouds that ride with the winds. Under certain temperature conditions, the water in these clouds is released, and it comes back to earth as rain or snow.

Thunderstorms have always been fascinating to man. In any

How does light travel? such storm, you see the flash of lightning before you hear the thunder. You see the lightning because the light travels faster than the sound. Light travels about 186,200 miles per second and sound about 1100 feet per second.

At this tremendous speed, the light from the sun, which is about 93,000,000 miles away, takes about eight minutes to reach us on earth. It is possible for us to see 93,000,000 miles away. But if you went to the top of a high mountain or tall building, how far away could you see? Certainly you would not be able to see the Pacific Ocean if you were atop either the Rocky Mountains in Wyoming or the Empire State Building in New York.

You can see the sun but cannot see far across the earth's surface because light waves travel in straight lines. They cannot go around a corner or around an object.

Look at a man walking down a street or

Why are there shadows? road in the sunlight and you will see his shadow. If you watch two men walking in the sunlight and carrying a six-foot pane of glass between them, you will see the shadow of each man six feet apart, but there will be no shadow of the pane of glass.

Shadows are easily explained since we know that light travels in a straight line. We also know that light waves pass through some bodies and not through others.

When light strikes a body and passes through it unchanged, we call such a body or material *transparent*. Most glass is such a material, especially window glass, and it is for this reason that we do not see the shadow of the window pane which the men are carrying. Do you know of any other transparent materials? The most common one, with which we are familiar, is air. Another is clear water.

On the other hand, some materials do not let light pass through them at all.

They stop the light waves just as you would catch a ball that was being thrown to someone standing behind you. Such materials are called *opaque*. Men's bodies, like steel, rock, concrete or even cardboard, are opaque and do not permit the light to pass through. An opaque body casts a shadow.

What materials scatter light? In addition to transparent and opaque materials, there is a third type of substance which is more like a transparent material than an opaque material. This type permits the light waves to pass through it, but unlike transparent materials, we cannot see through these materials. They scatter the light rays rather than permitting them to pass through unchanged.

These materials are known as *translucent*. Frosted glass, like that used for frosted light bulbs, is translucent. Other examples are very thin cloths or paper, such as waxed paper. Take a piece of waxed paper and hold it between you and a lighted electric lamp. You will see the light shining through the waxed paper, but you will be unable to see the lamp. This is because the waxed paper scatters the light. This scattering of light is known as *diffusion*.

Why do shadows vary in size? When a light shines on an opaque object, that object casts a shadow. Maybe you have noticed that sometimes your shadow is very big and other times it is small. When you are out in the sunlight at

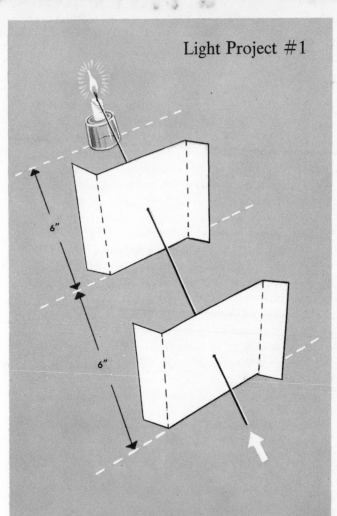

HOW TO DEMONSTRATE THAT LIGHT TRAVELS IN A STRAIGHT LINE

To do this experiment you need two large pieces of cardboard and a long straight wire or knitting needle and a candle.

Bend both pieces of cardboard as shown and make a small hole in each piece of cardboard. Punch the hole in both pieces of cardboard at the same time so that both holes are exactly in the same position on each piece.

Light the candle and line up both pieces of cardboard as shown in the sketch so that the first piece is six inches away from the candle and the second cardboard six inches from the first. Set the candle on a glass so that when you are looking through the small holes, you see the flame of the candle.

If you slip the knitting needle or wire through both holes, it will reach the flame of the candle; use a metal knitting needle so it won't burn and take it out of the flame quickly before the metal gets hot. The straight wire or needle is the path of the light.

Now if you remove the wire or needle and move the cardboard nearest you to one side or the other and again look through the holes, you will be unable to see the flame directly — proof that light travels in a straight line.

HOW TO EXPERIMENT WITH SHADOWS

Cut a circular disc of cardboard a little bit smaller than the size of the lens of a flashlight. Attach the cardboard to a short, thin stick. Stand about a foot away from any wall in a dark room so that your right side is facing the wall. Hold the flashlight in your left hand; turn it on and shine it at the wall. Now, in your right hand, hold the stick attached to the cardboard disc and place the disc about a foot away from the flashlight. The shadow of the cardboard on the wall is about the same size as the cardboard itself. Now cut a circular disc of cardboard about twice as large as the lens of the flashlight, and attach it to a thin stick. Stand in the same position with the wall on your right and the lighted flashlight in your left hand shining on the wall. Place the larger cardboard disc about a foot away from the light, between the flashlight and wall. Now you will notice that the shadow is much larger than the piece of cardboard.

If the object is larger than the light source, its shadow will be much larger than its real size. Similarly, an object smaller than the light source, at the same distance from the light, will cast a shadow much smaller than its real size, and an object of equal size at the same distance, will cast a shadow of equal size.

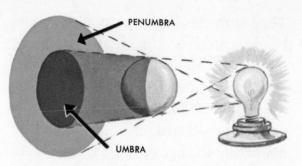

A tiny light ray, that would pass through a small hole in a cardboard, will produce a uniformly dark shadow when an opaque object is placed in its path. When the source of light is larger, however, such as an electric bulb, the sun, or even a candle, we often find multiple shadows. One shadow is dark and sharply defined, while the other is indistinct and blurry. The center or dark, sharp shadow is known as the *umbra,* caused when all of the light waves in this area are stopped. The blurry, indistinct shadow is known as the penumbra, and this lighter shadow is created because not all the light has been completely stopped by the opaque object.

Light Project #2

noontime, you will find that your shadow is small; but late in the afternoon, your shadow is much larger. Thus, we have one of the first rules about shadows: the size or length of the shadow depends upon the angle at which the light strikes the object. The size of the shadow is also influenced by the size of the source of light and the size of the opaque object.

Shadows used to help people tell the time of day before clocks were invented and even for a long while before clocks and watches were commonly used. They used a sundial to tell the time of day; in fact some people still use sundials but mainly for decoration in their gardens. The time of day was "read" from the sundial, just as we read time by looking at the hands of a clock. They could read the sundial either by the length of the shadow or the position of the shadow.

Hold this book close to a table lamp and the pages will appear bright and easy to read. But as you walk away from the light, holding the book in your hand, the pages become dimmer and more difficult to read if there are no other lights in the room. The brightness of the page in the book is called *illumination* and it depends upon the amount of light reflected by the page.

Why do lights look dimmer far away?

Illumination depends upon both the brightness of the source of light and the distance between the light and the surface receiving the light. Scientists have a formula to express the relationship between the distance and amount of illumination. It is known as the "Law of Inverse Square."

According to this scientific rule, the amount of illumination decreases very quickly the farther we are from the source of light. For example, a book held *one* foot away from the light receives four times as much illumination as a book held *two* feet away from the light. Four feet from the light, the illumination is only one-sixteenth the amount of light received one foot from the light.

In other words, if we wanted the same

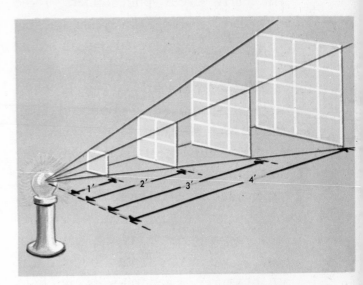

Illumination decreases very fast with distance.

amount of illumination on the book two feet from the light, as there was on the book one foot away, we would need a light that is four times as bright as the original light.

SUNDIAL

The Bending of Light

The image in the mirror shows right and left reversed.

The early Greek philosophers, some 3,000 years ago, be-

Why are objects visible?

lieved that an object is visible to us because our eyes send out special rays, and that when these rays bounced off an object and returned to our eyes, we would see the object. Today, we know that our eyes do not send out the rays but instead receive the rays emitted by the object. We have already seen that these rays can be two types: (a) direct light, as we receive from a body that is a light source or generates its own light waves, such as the sun; and (b) indirect light, as we receive when a body reflects light, just as this page reflects the light by which we are reading. The body that produces its own light waves, like the sun or an electric bulb, is said to be *luminous*, while a body that reflects light, such as the moon or this page, is said to be illuminated. Thus, any object that sends light waves toward our eyes is visible.

You have frequently seen your reflection in a mirror, on

How are light waves reflected?

a polished table or in a window pane.

These reflections exist because the light waves strike these surfaces and bounce off in much the same manner as a ball thrown against a wall.

While you would have little difficulty in distinguishing between your reflection and yourself when looking in a mirror, the scientist is careful to use specific terms or words to make this distinction. The reflection you see is known as a *reflected or mirror image,* while you or the actual object — a lamp in the room, a table, etc. — is referred to as the real object.

The mirror image or reflection we see, when looking into a mirror, is *symmetrical;* that is, everything facing the mirror appears to be repeated behind the mirror at the same distance as the original object is in front of it. Everything is the same, except for one thing: in the mirror image right and left are reversed. If you face a mirror and raise your right hand, the reflected image appears to raise its left hand.

If you have already tried Light Project #1, page 7, you

How can we make light turn a corner?

have proved for yourself that light travels in a straight line. We make use of this fact when we want to make light turn a corner. This is done by reflection.

The periscope, similar to that used in

a submarine or that used in a space capsule by an astronaut, makes use of the principle of reflection. Light is made to change its normal straight-line course by being reflected off a mirror or special surface. It is possible to control the direction of the reflected light because we know the "Law of Reflection."

According to this law or rule, if a light wave strikes a surface from which it will be reflected at an angle, it will "bounce off" at an angle. The light wave that strikes the surface is known as the *incident ray*. The angle between

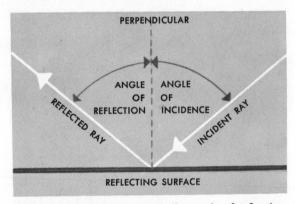

The angle of incidence equals the angle of reflection.

HOW TO DECODE "SECRET MESSAGES" WITH A MIRROR

As you remember from the previous section, mirror images are reversed. You can use this to decode "secret messages."

To write your message in code, place a piece of carbon paper, with the carbon side up, on the table and lay a piece of plain paper over it. Use the rounded edge of a toothpick or a pointed stick as a code "pencil." Write your message across the paper. You will see nothing on the top, but when you lift the paper, you will find that there is writing on the back of it.

To "decode" this secret message, you have to hold it in front of a mirror. Since the mirror reverses the image, the message is now as legible as if it were written the normal way.

Light Project #3 ➡

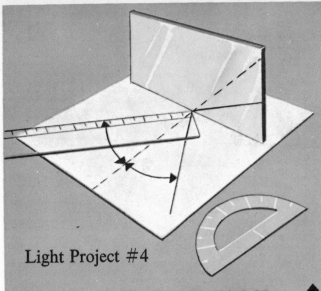

Light Project #4

HOW TO MEASURE THE ANGLE OF REFLECTION

We know that if we throw a ball straight at a wall, it will bounce straight back, and if we throw it at an angle, it will bounce off at an angle. This is known as the *Law of Reflection*. It also works for light.

All you need to test this law is: a mirror, a protractor, a pencil and a piece of paper.

1. Draw a dashed line on the paper and then draw a solid line to meet one end, so that they form an angle smaller than a right angle.
2. Take the mirror and place it at the point where the two lines join so that the dashed line on the paper and its reflection in the mirror appear as a continuous straight line.
3. Looking into the mirror, line up one edge of the ruler with the reflection of the solid line. Draw this line with your pencil.
4. Measure the angles on each side of the dashed line with the protractor. The two angles will be equal.
5. Try this several times, changing the size of the angle each time. The two angles will always be the same.

MIRROR

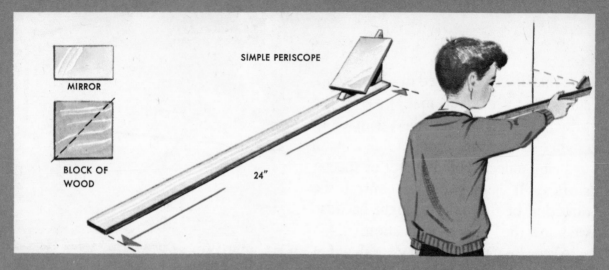

MIRROR

BLOCK OF
WOOD

SIMPLE PERISCOPE

24"

Light Project #5

HOW TO MAKE A PERISCOPE

The simplest periscope requires only a small mirror, a stick about two feet long and a small block of wood. Cut the block so that each edge is as long as the mirror. Next, cut the block in half, cutting along a line joining diagonally opposite corners.

Attach half the block to the end of the stick and glue the mirror on the block as shown. You can now hold the stick and project the mirror section and see around a corner.

An enclosed periscope can be made by using two small mirrors, about 2 by 3 inches, the size ladies use in their handbags, and a piece of cardboard 8 inches wide and about 24 inches long. Measure off the distance shown in the diagram. Cut off the excess cardboard (shaded area); cut two one-inch circles as shown; then bend the rest of the board along the drawn lines.

The mirrors are held in place with cellophane tape and all of the edges of the periscope are also held together with cellophane tape.

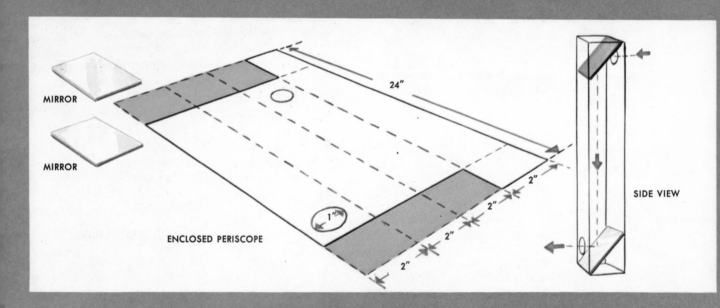

MIRROR

MIRROR

24"

2"

2"

2"

2"

1"

2"

ENCLOSED PERISCOPE

SIDE VIEW

the incident ray and a perpendicular drawn to the surface is known as the *angle of incidence*. The light wave that has bounced off the reflecting surface is called the *reflected ray* and the angle between this ray and the perpendicular is known as the *angle of reflection*. In every case, the angle of incidence is equal to the angle of reflection, as you can see when you try Light Project #4, "How to measure the angle of reflection," on this page.

The Law of Reflection is true under all conditions,

What is diffused reflection?

whether the surface is smooth, like a mirror, or rough, like a sandy beach or a brick wall. If you took a flashlight on a moonless night and pointed it at a very smooth varnished wood exterior wall of a house, the light would be reflected. If the light were aimed at an angle to the wall, the angle of incidence would be equal to the angle of reflection.

However, when light strikes a rough surface, the light is diffused. The reason the light from a flashlight would not bounce off a rough brick wall as it did from a smooth wood wall, is that the light is sent off in different directions by the uneven surface. Yet, if we could examine each minute portion of the light — break the beam up into many individual light waves — we would find that in each case the law of reflection worked. But because the surface is made up of many small portions at different angles, each small light wave is reflected in a different direction.

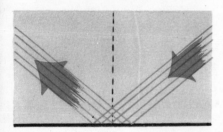

If light strikes a smooth surface, the reflection is regular.

If light strikes a rough surface the reflection will be diffused.

Why does light bend in transparent materials?

As you remember, we noted at the beginning of this book, that light waves travel through space and certain kinds of materials.

You observe refraction when you see a spoon or a straw in a glass of water. When you go spear fishing, you have to calculate the same refraction or you may miss your target.

We also found that when light waves go through a material, we say that the material is transparent. But light does not travel at the same speed through all materials; it goes slower through some than through others.

While light waves travel the most quickly through air, they go much slower through water and even slower through glass. When the light waves, traveling through the air, strike water or glass at an angle, they bend as they slow down. Scientists describe this bending by saying: "when light passes from one transparent medium (such as air,

13

water or glass) to another at an angle, the light waves are bent at the boundary between the two mediums." This bending is known as *refraction*.

You can see this easily if you put a straw in a transparent glass of water. The straw appears to be bent at the point where it enters the water.

This bending or refraction takes place every time the light wave passes from one medium to the next as long as the light passes the boundary between the two mediums at an angle. It takes place when light passes from the air into glass, and it takes place again when the light waves pass from the glass into the air. Refraction also takes place between air and water, water and air, water and glass, and glass and water.

There is always some moisture in the atmosphere, but when this amount increases substantially, it affects the light waves. Light traveling through space goes at a much faster speed than light waves passing through very moist air near the surface of the earth. Space and moist air are considered by scientists as two different mediums, just as water and glass are different. And just as light waves are refracted as they pass from air into glass or water, the light waves from space are refracted when they pass through the moist air.

What happens to light in hot moist air?

You can see this refraction at work if you watch the sun setting on a very humid, warm day. Just as the sun nears the horizon, the previously round disk seems to have a flattened bottom; it is not a perfect circle. The light waves

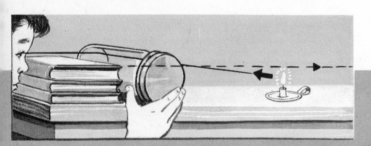

HOW TO PROVE THAT THE AIR BENDS SUNLIGHT

In the morning we actually see the sun before it comes over the horizon and in the evening, we see the sun after it has passed below the horizon. This is another example of refraction since the air around the earth bends the rays of the sun and makes us see the sun where it isn't located. You can try an experiment in your own home to see how this works. All you need is a large jar with a cover, a candle and several books.

Set the empty jar on its side and place several books one atop the other next to the jar until they are about two-thirds as high as the jar. Now take the books and place them along one edge of a table.

Light Project #6

About 24 inches from the same edge, place a very short candle in a dish or holder; the candle should be about half as high as the pile of books.

Fill the jar with water and put the cap on tightly. Now light the candle and you are ready to see how the air bends the sun's rays. The candle represents the sun and the jar of water is the air around the earth.

If you bend down so that you can look just even with the top of the books, you should be unable to see the flame on the candle. (If you do, shorten the candle.) Now, set the jar on its side alongside the books, between the books and the candle. If you sight along the top edge of the books, you will now be able to see the flame of the candle. The water in the jar has bent the light waves from the candle's flame toward you, just as the atmosphere bends the light waves from the sun before they reach your eyes.

coming from the bottom portion of the sun are refracted by the moisture in the air to create this optical illusion.

Frequently, when you are driving along

Why does a dry road look wet? a turnpike or thruway on a clear, hot day, you see what appear to be pools of water on the highway up ahead. However, as you come closer, you find that the road surface that seemed wet before is actually dry. If you look ahead, there are the pools of water again; they seem to be moving in the same direction as the car.

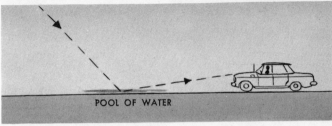

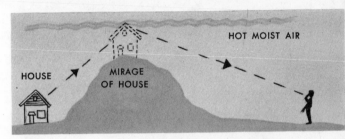

The pools of water you see in the road ahead on a sunny day disappear as you come close to them.

Actually, there are no pools of water on the road at all. Those watery images are an illusion, a mirage, such as occurs in the desert or even on the water of a large lake or the ocean.

These pools of water, or any mirage for that matter, occur only under certain conditions. First, it is necessary to have a relatively flat surface, such as a roadway, water or sand. Secondly, you must be able to see a considerable distance over the flat surface.

Most important is the presence of a layer of hot, moist air on an otherwise perfectly clear day. This hot moisture-ladened layer of air immediately over the surface acts like a reflective surface, just as calm water does on a pond. Thus, as we look in the distance at a roadway, we will see the sky reflected by the layer immediately above the road. The reflection of the sky will make that portion of the roadway appear different from the other portions of the road; it will look like small pools of water.

Single mirages (above) and double mirages (below) have fooled many travelers in the desert but are not limited to this location.

Sometimes, because of wind currents and air masses, a hot moist layer of air can be overhead. It may be exceedingly thin or it can extend upwards for a number of miles. The most important thing is that the air nearest the ground is cooler than that higher up. In this case, the hot layer again can act as a reflective surface. Light from a source many miles away can be reflected downward, causing a person on the ground to see what is commonly known as a mirage.

15

WHY DOES THE MOON LOOK BIGGER WHEN IT RISES?

When we watch the moon come over the horizon, it often appears enormously large, only to become smaller and smaller as it rises in the sky and passes overhead. This is sometimes caused by refraction in much the same way as the sun appears to be flattening when it sets.

On warm moist nights, the air with the water in it causes the light from the moon to be refracted. The light waves bend as they pass through the moist air and produce one of the many optical illusions that our eyes play on us.

The illusion is most obvious when the moon is close to the surface of the earth or near the horizon; we see it behind tall trees or buildings and we are able to make a size comparison. Our eyes are unable to adjust for the true distance of the moon from the trees and buildings and we make our comparison as if the moon were merely a little way behind the trees. The thousands of miles to the moon are compressed by our eyes. However, after the moon rises, we have no object with which to compare its size.

Nevertheless, you can satisfy your own curiosity as a scientist by "measuring" the moon as it comes over the horizon and as it climbs high into the sky. Take a clear piece of plastic and hold it at arm's length between your eyes and the moon. Mark the plastic in crayon so that you have a circle the same size as the image of the moon. Later, when the moon is high in the heaven, view the moon again through the plastic. You will be surprised to see that the circle you drew before is still just the size of the image of the moon.

Magic with Light

For ages magicians have fascinated audiences by putting the laws of reflection and refraction to use. The famous carnival magic trick of making a performer's head appear on a table while the rest of his body "disappears," is possible because of the magic that can be performed by light.

How can you make things invisible?

Let's review the basic idea of refraction so that we can understand how it is done. Remember that light waves leaving one medium and striking another at an angle, will bend as they travel through the second medium; that is, they will still travel in a straight line but in a direction different from the original one. Thus, when light passing through air enters water at an angle, the light wave will bend. Similarly, if that light wave completes its journey through the water and re-enters the air, that light wave will again change its direction because it bends as it passes from one medium to the next.

Thus, we can try some magic by putting a penny in the center at the bottom of a large opaque bowl. Look across the top edge of the bowl so that you cannot see the penny. While you stay in this position, have someone pour water into the bowl. Suddenly, as if by magic, you can see the coin which you could not see before. You see it because of the refraction of light.

But we started out to make things invisible, didn't we? Well, this previous trick was reverse magic—making something visible which wasn't visible, by using the bending of light waves. Now, let's make something invisible. This time we again place a penny in the center at the bottom of a large bowl, and we add water to the bowl at once.

If you look straight down into the bowl, you'll see the penny. Now start to move your head lower by bending your knees so that your eyes will eventually be looking over the edge of the bowl. As you move your head lower and still look at the penny, that penny appears to be moving. The penny looks as if it is climbing up the other side of the bowl. Then suddenly, as you're bending your knees more and more, the penny "disappears;" it looks as if it climbed out of the bowl and vanished in the air.

Another trick with light involves the use of a white-enameled funnel. Drill a small hole, 1/8 inch in diameter about halfway down from the top. Insert a clear glass rod, such as a drink mixer, through the narrow end of the funnel so that it projects about one-third the way into the funnel.

Hold the funnel and glass rod directly below a bright ceiling light. Peek through the small hole in the side. The overhead light will be reflected within the funnel and the glass rod will be invisible.

Light Project # 8

Actually, as you move your eyes lower toward the edge of the bowl, the angle of refraction increases. It finally reaches a point where the surface of the water acts as a reflector, or just like a mirror, so that it is no longer possible to see the penny. This particular angle, the one at which the penny disappears from view, is known as the *critical angle*.

Have you ever watched a movie or a television show where the wheels of a speeding automobile or an airplane taking off appear to be turning backward?

Why do forward moving wheels sometimes appear to be turning backward?

To understand this strange optical effect, you must realize that a motion picture film projected on the screen consists of a series of individual pictures. The pictures are joined together so that you can see one after another, but there is a very small time, a fraction of a second, between each frame or picture when the screen is completely dark.

Each individual picture shows the au-

tomobile or airplane moving along the road or the airfield. However, if the wheel does not make a complete turn from one still picture to the next, it looks as if the wheel is moving backward. For example, if we watch the top edge of the wheel in one picture and if that top edge does not make a complete turn, but instead completes three-

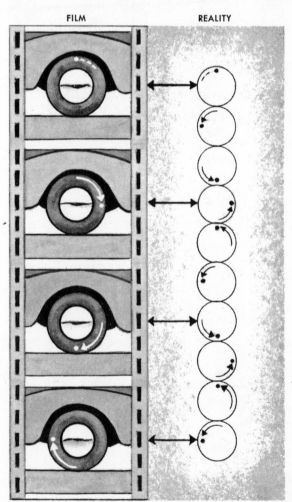

The illustration demonstrates the stroboscopic effect.

18

fourths of a turn, it looks as if the wheel turned one-fourth backward. Now, in the third picture, with the wheel making only three-fourths of a turn, the top edge visible in the first picture is directly on the bottom. Again it appears as if the wheel has turned one-fourth backward. Thus, the automobile continues moving forward and wheels continue to appear to be going backward. This is known as the *stroboscopic effect*.

You can see this stroboscopic effect by using the accompanying diagram of the six concentric circles with the white

The wheels will turn!

gear in the middle. Hold the illustration at about arm's length away from you and concentrate on the circles. Hold one hand still and with the other shift the book up and down vertically, about two or three inches in each direction. Notice that the inside of the circles appears to be turning.

Have you noticed anything else? Yes? The gear inside the group of circles appears to be turning in the opposite direction of the circles. This is the same effect as we see when watching a car or train on the movie screen. It is the stroboscopic effect once again.

HOW TO MAKE A STROBOSCOPE

You can test the stroboscopic effect of light by making a simple stroboscope using a piece of cardboard four inches square and a small hand drill.

Cut the cardboard into a circle four inches in diameter. Divide the circle into eight equal pie-shaped sections. You can do this by drawing a line through the center of the circle and then drawing another at right angles through it; this divides the circle into four parts. If you divide each fourth into halves, you will have eight sections. Leave one section white and color the next, until you have four white sections and four colored sections.

Force a nail through the center of the circle so that the cardboard cannot turn unless you turn the nail. Insert the nail into the chuck of the drill. Now, holding the drill so that the circle faces you, turn the handle of the drill.

Because there are many types of hand drills, it is not possible to tell you exactly how fast to turn the handle. Try turning at varying speeds until you find the speed at which it will appear as if the disc is standing perfectly still.

Once you have found this speed, you will find that if you turn the handle just a little bit slower, the segments of the disc will appear to be turning backwards. Then as you increase the speed, the segments will appear to be standing still, and finally, as you turn even faster, the segments will move forward rapidly.

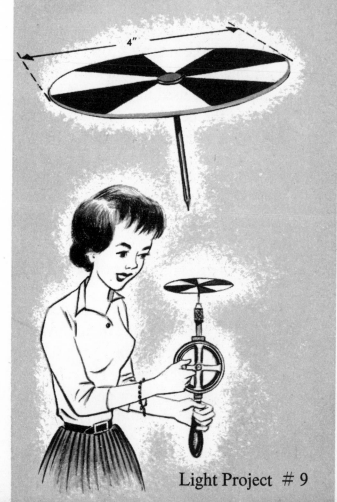

Light Project # 9

MULTIPLE IMAGES

The smaller the angle of the two mirrors becomes or when a third mirror is used, the faster the money "grows."

Every time light waves are reflected, we produce another reflected or mirror image. If you have ever been in a store where they have three mirrors so that you can see how you look in a new suit or dress, you will find that you can see three images of yourself and some times even more, depending upon the angle at which you look into the mirrors. You can use mirrors to "make money grow." Try this with only one penny and two mirrors, such as those used in a pocketbook.

How are multiple images created?

Place the penny on a table and hold the two mirrors edge to edge so that all you see is a single reflection. Now, keeping the touching edges together, move the outside edges of both mirrors toward you. The closer the mirrors come together, the more images or reflections of the penny you see.

At first, you see a reflection of the penny in each mirror; then as the mirrors reflect into each other, you see four reflections plus the original penny—you now see five pennies. Now keep turning the mirrors, making sure that the touching edges are together, and that the outside edges practically touch the penny. Then you will see six reflections plus the real penny.

Lenses and Optics

Just a few pages ago, we saw how we could make things invisible by refracting or reflecting light waves. The refracting of light waves as they pass from one substance to another—from air to glass and then again from glass to air—helps us make objects appear bigger or closer than they really are, or can help us make objects appear farther away.

What is a lens?

To do this we use lenses. A lens is a curved piece of glass that is used to

The number of images becomes infinite when the two mirrors face each other and are parallel to each other.

refract light waves, either concentrating them or dispersing the waves, depending upon the shape of the glass. While lenses have been made of glass for several centuries, today we also use special clear plastic to make lenses since the plastic lenses do not break as easily as those made of glass.

Essentially, there are three basic forms or shapes of lenses, although you will find many variations

How are lenses shaped?

of each and, at times, even a combination of the basic shapes.

The *prism* or triangular shaped piece of glass is one form of a lens. If you look at this lens from its side, it would be shaped somewhat like a wedge of pie.

Another basic shape of a lens is *convex*. A side view of such a lens would reveal that it is thicker at its center than at its edge. If you picture two parentheses, such as ( ), so that they are in their proper order as we would use them when writing, you would have the shape of a convex lens by joining the tops.

The third basic shape of a lens is *concave*. When viewed from its side, this

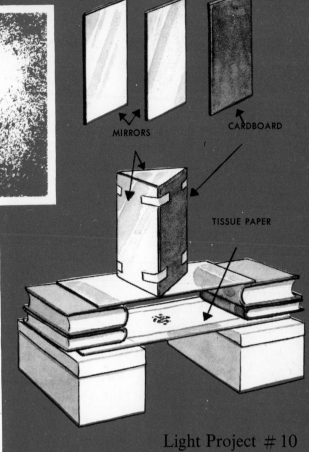

Light Project # 10

HOW TO MAKE A KALEIDOSCOPE

For centuries, people have been fascinated by the kaleidoscope. The word means "beautiful form" in old Greek. It is a simple device to make multiple images.

To make one yourself, you need two mirrors exactly the same shape and size and a piece of cardboard to match. Stand the mirrors and the cardboard on their shorter edges in the form of a triangle with the mirrors facing the inside. You can hold the three pieces together with rubber bands or cellophane tape; cut a small piece of waxed paper to fit over one end and tape it into position.

Cut some very small pieces of colored tissue paper about the size of a pencil eraser, or you can use small chips of transparent colored plastic or glass. Set these on a piece of glass about ten inches above the table top; you can rest the glass on books or boxes. Use a shiny surface table or place an electric light under the glass.

Holding the mirror and cardboard triangle about two inches above the colored tissue or glass, look down through the top. You will see the many reflections of these small pieces. Actually, you will see six reflections plus the original of each little piece on the sheet of glass. By moving the small particles around on the glass, you can create many different patterns.

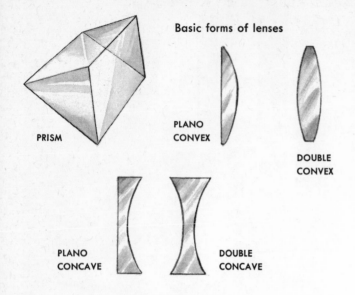

Basic forms of lenses

PRISM

PLANO CONVEX

DOUBLE CONVEX

PLANO CONCAVE

DOUBLE CONCAVE

lens is thinner at its center than at either end. If you picture two parentheses in the opposite way from that which they are normally used, such as)(, you would have the shape of a concave lens.

In studying lenses and how they refract light, it is best to review the path of a light wave as it passes through a piece of

How does light pass through a prism?

The path of light striking a windowpane at an angle and perpendicular.

GLASS

LIGHT RAY PERPENDICULAR

ORIGINAL PATH

LIGHT RAY AT AN ANGLE

GLASS

LIGHT RAY DISPLACED

glass, such as a window pane. The light wave may take either of two paths depending upon the angle at which it strikes the flat piece of glass.

If the light wave strikes perpendicular to the surface of the glass, that is at right angles to the surface, then the wave will pass through the glass unchanged. However, if the light wave strikes the glass' surface at an angle, it will be refracted. First, it is refracted as it passes from the air into the glass, that is, its direction is changed. Secondly, when the light wave leaves the glass and passes into the air, it is again refracted. Actually, the light will pass through the glass, coming out at the same angle at which it entered, but the path will be shifted over slightly. This shift in position of the path is known as *displacement*.

Similarly, when a light wave enters and leaves a prism, it is refracted. Let's trace the light wave's path since its refraction in a prism will help you to understand how light passes through the other two types of lenses as well.

First, let us consider the prism itself. A prism is usually a solid piece of glass, shaped as though you had taken a triangle and extended it backwards. In other words, a prism has two triangular bases at each end, and the three sides between the bases have the form of parallelograms. For purposes of a diagram, however, it is only necessary to see a triangle, which is actually a cross section of the prism. A wave can strike the prism either perpendicular to one of the sides or at an angle.

If the light wave strikes perpendicular

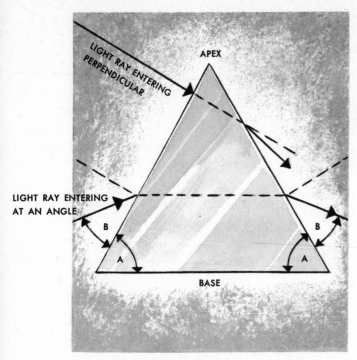

The path of light going through a prism.

If we look at a concave or convex lens from its side, we can draw an imaginary line from the top to bottom of the lens; this is known as the *axis* of the lens. At right angles to this axis and passing through the exact center of the lens is another imaginary line, known as the *principal axis*. In addition, any imaginary line we draw at any angle to the lens that passes through the center of the lens is known as the *secondary axis*.

How does light pass through convex and concave lenses?

Scientists have found that any light

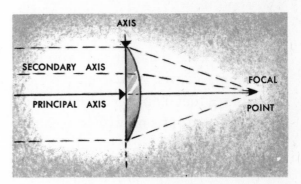

Identification of the major parts of a lens.

to the side, it will continue in the same path until it reaches the other side of the prism just before it is ready to pass from the glass into the air. At this point it is emerging at an angle to the air. Because it is striking the air at an angle, it will be refracted or bent.

On the other hand, if the light wave strikes the side at an angle, it will be refracted as it enters the glass. When it emerges on the other side of the prism — as it passes from the glass into the air — it is striking the air at an angle and will again be refracted. Scientists have found that the path at which the light wave leaves the prism is at the same angle with the base as the angle of the path at which it entered. Therefore, by knowing the angle at which the light wave will strike the prism, it is possible to determine the exact path at which it will leave.

wave traveling along either the principal axis or any secondary axis of a lens, passes through the lens unchanged; its path is continued without interruption. However, any light wave that strikes the lens along any other path is reflected by the lens.

Actually, more than one light wave originates from any object, just as a pebble dropped in a pond creates more than one wave in the water.

This is true whether the object is luminous, that is, the originating light source like a light bulb, or illuminated,

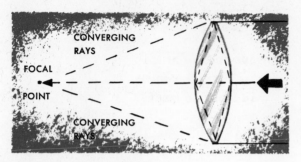

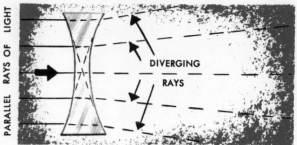

PATH OF LIGHT IN A CONVEX LENS

PATH OF LIGHT IN A CONCAVE LENS

that is, reflecting light from a light source like this page of the book.

Let us examine what happens to these light waves that strike a lens along any path other than the principal or secondary axis.

The convex lens is also known as a *converging lens* since the light waves that pass through it converge or bunch together toward the center. If you look at a simple convex lens from the side, you will see that it appears to be a modification of two prisms with a common base. As the light waves pass through a prism, they are bent or refracted toward the base. Thus, the light rays passing through the top and bottom imaginary prisms of a convex lens are bent toward the center or converge.

Similarly, a simple concave lens can be regarded as a combination of two prisms which are joined at their tops or apexes. Since the light waves passing through a prism are refracted toward the base, we can see that the concave lens spreads the light waves away from its center. This bending outward of light rays is known as *divergence*.

How does a lens form an image?

If you hold a piece of paper in one hand and an ordinary reading glass (a convex lens) in the other so that the glass is between a window and the paper, you will see an *image* of the outside scene on the paper. As you move the reading glass closer or farther away from the paper, you will find that the image is clearest at one specific distance. When the image is clearest, the distance from the reading

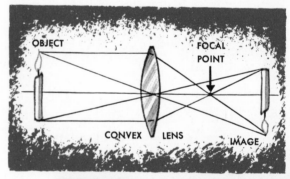

A simple reading glass can bring the "outside" into your room.

24

glass to the paper is the *focal length* of the lens.

This moving of the reading glass (lens) back and forth to obtain the sharpest possible image is exactly what we do when we focus a camera. We move the lens of the camera back and forth so that it will produce the sharpest image on the film.

You will notice something unusual about the image produced by the reading glass on the paper you are holding. It is upside down. The reason for this is that the lens *inverts* the scene when it produces an image, as is illustrated in the accompanying diagram.

How does science use lenses?

Without the use of lenses many great scientific discoveries and much of our scientific knowledge would not be possible. We use lenses in optical instruments, such as the microscope and telescope, to refract light and make objects appear larger than they do to the unaided eye. A microscope makes visible objects which the

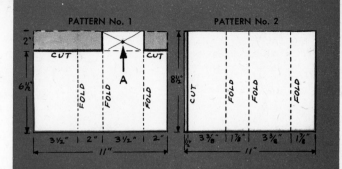

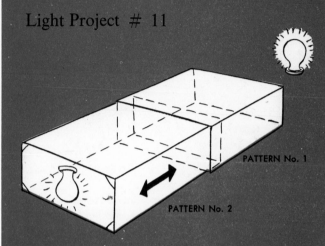

Light Project # 11

HOW TO MAKE A CAMERA OBSCURA

A very small pinhole acts the same as a convex lens and produces an inverted image. You can make a pinhole camera, also known as a camera obscura, with the following materials:

Two pieces of heavy cardboard, each about 8½ x 11 inches;

Some masking tape or cellophane tape;

a piece of household waxed paper or tracing paper about 3 x 4 inches.

To make the camera, cut one piece of cardboard following pattern #1. Make a very small pinhole — the sharp end of a safety pin should be adequate — at point "A" in the diagram. Fold along the lines indicated and tape the edges together carefully with cellophane or masking tape. Make certain that the edges are tightly sealed so that no light can enter.

Now, cut the other piece of cardboard following pattern #2. Fold along the lines indicated and join with tape. Cut the waxed paper so that it fits over one end of this part of the camera, leaving a very small triangle open at each edge and tape it.

To use the camera, insert the part with the waxed paper end into the part in which you made the pinhole as shown; hold the waxed paper part close to your eyes, staying in a shady place outdoors, or if you are inside the house, stay away from direct sunlight. Aim the pinhole at a light or bright, sunny place. Move the inside portion of your camera back and forth slowly until the scene appears sharply on the waxed paper screen.

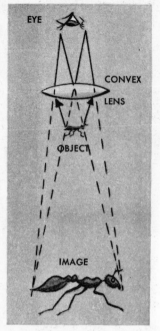

A SIMPLE MICROSCOPE

EYE

CONVEX LENS

OBJECT

IMAGE

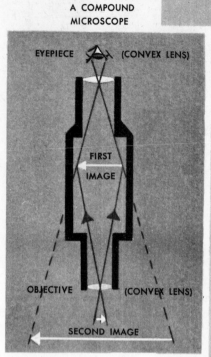

A COMPOUND MICROSCOPE

EYEPIECE (CONVEX LENS)

FIRST IMAGE

OBJECTIVE (CONVEX LENS)

SECOND IMAGE

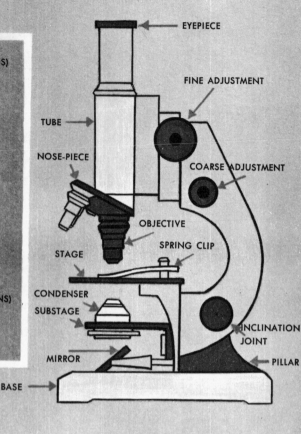

EYEPIECE

FINE ADJUSTMENT

TUBE

NOSE-PIECE

COARSE ADJUSTMENT

OBJECTIVE

SPRING CLIP

STAGE

CONDENSER

SUBSTAGE

INCLINATION JOINT

MIRROR

PILLAR

BASE

Without the use of lenses many discoveries made with the help of the microscope would not have been possible, because there would not be a microscope.

eye could not ordinarily see. We are able to study blood cells and minute plant and animal life, such as bacteria, and thus combat disease.

Lenses are also used in our study of space and the universe. The telescope brings distant stars and planets closer to earth by making them appear larger than they do to the naked eye.

Generally, several lenses, and often different types of lenses are used in combination in these scientific instruments. When we use only a single lens, such as a reading glass, we refer to the glass as a simple lens. When we use two or more lenses, the optical instrument is called "compound." A compound microscope is illustrated here.

By using several lenses to refract the light, it is possible to enlarge an object many many times. Modern optical mi-

croscopes can enlarge an object up to 2,400 times. A single period (.) on this page magnified that many times would appear to be the size of a disk with a 10-foot diameter.

If you have tried to obtain an image of an outdoor scene using the reading glass and plain paper as previously described, or if you have made and experimented with the *camera obscura* (page 25), you have seen how you obtain an inverted image of the scene. In other words, the lens turns everything upside down.

How is the eye like a camera's lens?

In many ways, our eyes act like a camera. Let us examine the camera first so that we can better understand how our eyes work.

In a camera there are four basic parts

or controls. First, there is the lens itself; the light rays pass through it to form the image on the film. Second, there is the film, a special material sensitive to light, which produces the picture when it is developed in chemicals. Third, there is a control that varies the amount of light that passes through the lens, thereby providing just the right amount of exposure for the film. Finally, the distance regulator varies the distance between the lens and film so that we can focus the camera and obtain the sharpest picture, depending upon the distance of the object from the camera.

If you look in the mirror, you see that your eye consists of a colored circle on a white background with a black circle in the center. The colored portion is the iris. The black center is the pupil, an adjustable opening behind which is the eye's lens. The light passes through this lens and is focused on the curved back of the eyeball, or the retina, which acts like the film in a camera.

If you are in a dimly lit room, you'll find that the pupil is large, but in the bright sunlight, your pupil is small. The amount of light entering the eye through the pupil is controlled by the iris, which is a circular muscle. Too much light passing through the pupil would harm the retina, while too little would make it impossible to see.

We focus a camera to obtain a sharper image by changing the distance between the lens and film; the lens of the eye does not work in the same way. If you could look inside the eye, you would find several special muscles attached to the lens. These muscles control the shape of the lens which is convex. By changing the shape of the lens — making it thicker or thinner at the center — we are able to change the focal length of the lens and thus adjust for the distance of the object we are looking at.

There is seemingly an important difference between the eye and the camera. We know that the image produced by

HOW TO MAKE A SIMPLE TELESCOPE

To make a telescope you will need two convex lenses and two different sizes of cardboard tubing. The cardboard tubing should be such that the smallest size just fits within the larger one and can be moved back and forth easily.

If the opening of the cardboard tubing is much bigger than the lenses, cut a piece of heavy cardboard to the same size as the tube opening. Now place one of the lenses so that the center of the lens is exactly over the center of this cardboard disc. Trace around the edge of the lens and cut out the center of the cardboard disc carefully. Now tape the cut cardboard disc over the end of the tubing. Then tape the lens over the opening you have cut.

You are to repeat this for the other lens, attaching it to a cardboard disc which is placed on the second tubing size. The length of the tubing depends upon

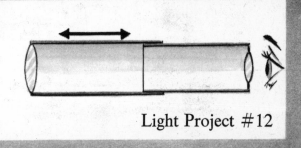

Light Project #12

the strength of the lenses you are using. It will be necessary to experiment with this, starting with each cardboard tube about 18 inches long, and cutting each down about 2 to 3 inches at a time.

You can determine the exact length by holding one lens in front of your eye and moving the inside tube back and forth until you see an enlarged image of the object you are looking at. Aim the tubes at an object about 10 or 15 feet away in order to determine the length of the tubes.

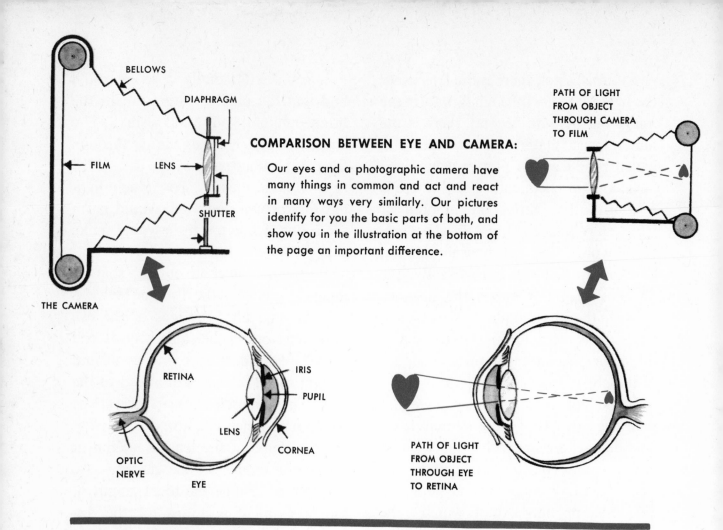

COMPARISON BETWEEN EYE AND CAMERA:

Our eyes and a photographic camera have many things in common and act and react in many ways very similarly. Our pictures identify for you the basic parts of both, and show you in the illustration at the bottom of the page an important difference.

BELLOWS

DIAPHRAGM

FILM

LENS

SHUTTER

THE CAMERA

PATH OF LIGHT FROM OBJECT THROUGH CAMERA TO FILM

RETINA

IRIS

PUPIL

LENS

CORNEA

OPTIC NERVE

EYE

PATH OF LIGHT FROM OBJECT THROUGH EYE TO RETINA

Just as in the camera, the object forms an inverted image on the retina of the human eye, but this image is turned right side up by the human mind.

the camera's lens is upside down. Yet, when we look at anything we see it right side up. You would no doubt ask if your eyes really invert the scene and produce an image that is upside down.

Actually, our eyes do produce an inverted image on the retina. However, knowing from experience that this is upside down, the image is adjusted by our brain which permits us to see things as they really are. This changing is solely the work of the mind which interprets what the optic nerve relays to it.

How much control our mind has over the interpretation of what our eyes see was demonstrated many years ago by a Swiss scientist. He tried an experiment in which several people wore special glasses. These glasses were convex lenses that turned the scene upside down just as the camera lens does. The eyes looking at the scenes upside down turned them right side up and this image was focused on the eye's retina. When the people first started to wear the glasses, they viewed everything right side up, but their brains, used to changing the message received from the eye's retina, inverted the scene. Thus, these people looked at the world upside down. However, after a few weeks of continually wearing these glasses, the mind, realizing that this was not the real world, suddenly accepted the images as they were received. The people wearing glasses saw everything right side up, just as if they were not wearing glasses. The mind adjusted to the changed situation. Then, when the glasses were removed, the mind, now taking the retina

image as true, caused these people without glasses to see things upside down. Again, after a short period of time, the mind readjusted and the people again saw normally.

Have your eyes regularly checked by a doctor. Lenses can correct faulty vision.

Why do people wear glasses? When you look at an object in the distance, the lenses of your eyes form images on the retinas. As you move the object nearer, the shape of the lens must change or the image will be formed behind the retina. The muscles around the lens squeeze it so that it becomes more curved or thicker at the center.

If the eye muscles are too strong or not strong enough, or if the lenses are not properly shaped, the eye is unable to make the necessary changes in focus or *accommodation,* as it is called.

If the lens is too curved, the image then formed is in front of the retina. This condition is known as nearsightedness. On the other hand, if the lens is not curved enough, the image is formed behind the retina. This condition is known as farsightedness.

This condition of the eyes can be corrected by using another lens to aid the lens of the eye. The type of lens used in

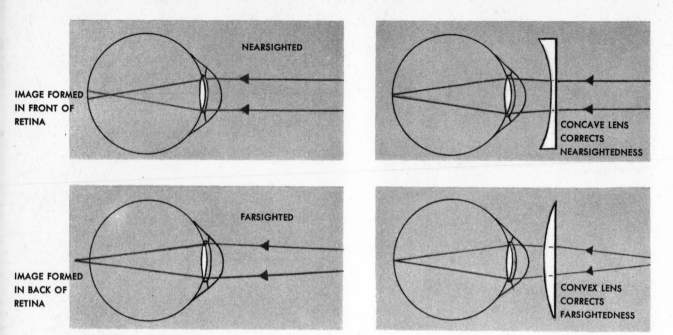

NEARSIGHTED

IMAGE FORMED IN FRONT OF RETINA

CONCAVE LENS CORRECTS NEARSIGHTEDNESS

FARSIGHTED

IMAGE FORMED IN BACK OF RETINA

CONVEX LENS CORRECTS FARSIGHTEDNESS

Concave spectacle lenses correct nearsightedness; convex lenses help overcome farsightedness.

eyeglasses depends upon whether the person is nearsighted or farsighted and to what degree.

The light image that passes through the pupil and lens of the eye is transmitted to the brain by the optic

What is your "blind spot?"

nerve. The point at which this nerve is attached to the retina is not sensitive to light; it is known as the *blind spot*.

You can find your own blind spot by using the accompanying blind spot test described below.

While we know that light travels very quickly, we must also remember that what we "see" is what our

What is an afterimage?

mind tells us we are looking at, and this involves more than the speed of light through the air. The light impulses received by the retina in the eyes are changed into nerve impulses and are transmitted to the brain by the optic nerves. These impulses also travel very quickly, taking a very small portion of a second to go from the eye to the brain. However, during that very small

HOW TO MAKE THE BLIND SPOT TEST

Close your left eye and hold this page at arm's length so that the X is directly in front of your right eye. You'll see the circle out of the corner of your eye. While you continue to look at the X, move the page very slowly toward you.

Somewhere along the way, when the image of the circle is formed on the blind spot of your eye, the circle will disappear. Then as you continue to move the page closer and closer, it will reappear.

You will find the same is true of the star. It too will disappear, but at a distance closer to you.

Light Project #13

time interval, the eyes may have shifted to another scene. While the new impulses are picked up by the retina, the old ones are still traveling to the brain. Thus, our brain tells us we are seeing something different from what our eyes are actually looking at.

You can try this yourself by looking at the illustration above. Concentrate on the drawing for one or two minutes; then quickly turn your head so that you are looking at a clear blank wall. What do you see? You see the drawing on the wall. This is known as an *afterimage*.

An optical illusion is the name we use **Do your eyes** to describe some-**ever betray you?** thing that we see with our eyes but which we know is not true. Remember earlier in this book the illusion of the full moon? It appeared bigger when it was just at the horizon than when it was high in the sky.

The accompanying illustrations include a number of the common optical illusions. These misinterpretations are due to a variety of causes, the most common of which are our lack of experience in viewing such scenes, carelessness and a physical timing factor.

The famous "which line is longer," is an example of carelessness, (See illustration, page 32). The upper line appears smaller because our eyes place the line's ends within the arrowheads rather than following the line to its tips.

Look at this diagram carefully and you will notice that where the white bands meet, shadows seem to flicker. It is an optical illusion created by the fact that any point away from the crossing of the white lines is surrounded by more black and looks brighter.

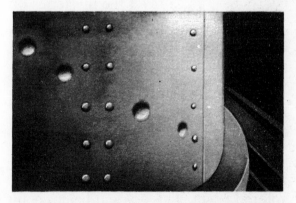

Turn the book upside down. How do the rivets and the dents appear now? Our eyes can fool us.

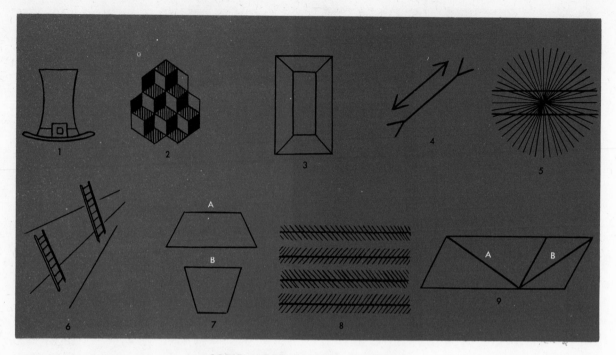

SOME MORE OPTICAL ILLUSIONS

Above are pictured a number of "famous" optical illusions. Test yourself and see how you score: 1. Is the hat as wide as it is high? 2. Count the cubes and then recount them carefully. 3. Look at the inside square; does it appear to shift back and forth? 4. Compare the length of the lines. Are they even in length? 5. Are the two horizontal lines curved or are they straight? 6. Which ladder is longer, or are they the same? 7. How does the length of lines A and B compare? 8. Are the horizontal lines parallel? 9. Compare the length of the diagonals A and B. Which one is longer or are they equal? Now take a ruler and measure to check your answers. Our eyes can fool us, as you can see.

Light and Color

It was not until about 300 years ago

What is "white light?"

that man began to unravel the mysteries of nature's colors. The experiments of the famous English scientist, Sir Isaac Newton, performed in 1665, are the basis for much of our knowledge of color. He found that when he passed a narrow beam of sunlight or "white light" through a triangular prism, the white light split into a multicolored beam. This colored beam, consisting of violet, indigo, blue, green, yellow, orange and red, is known as a *spectrum.*

Newton also discovered two other important facts about light and color. First, he found that he could not break any of the colors of the spectrum down into another group of colors as he had done with white light. He also found that he could pass the color spectrum through another triangular prism and produce white light. Thus, it was Newton who first discovered that white light is a combination of all the colors.

HOW TO MAKE A RAINBOW

The rainbow is nature's color spectrum. It always appears in one particular portion of the sky and only when you are facing away from the sun. The top of the rainbow is about halfway between the horizon and a point directly above your head. Furthermore, the sky behind the rainbow is always hazy or cloudy. It is the clouds or haze that make the rainbow possible.

The haze or clouds consist of millions of small drops of water and each of these drops acts as a prism breaking the reflected sunlight into a spectrum. Each drop reflects only a single color wave of the spectrum directly to our eyes, the color depending upon the height of the drop above the horizon.

You can make your own rainbow by placing a large piece of white paper on the floor in front of a window through which the bright sun is shining. Set a glass full of water on the window sill so that it extends slightly over the inside edge. The water in the glass will act as a prism and produce a spectrum on the paper on the floor.

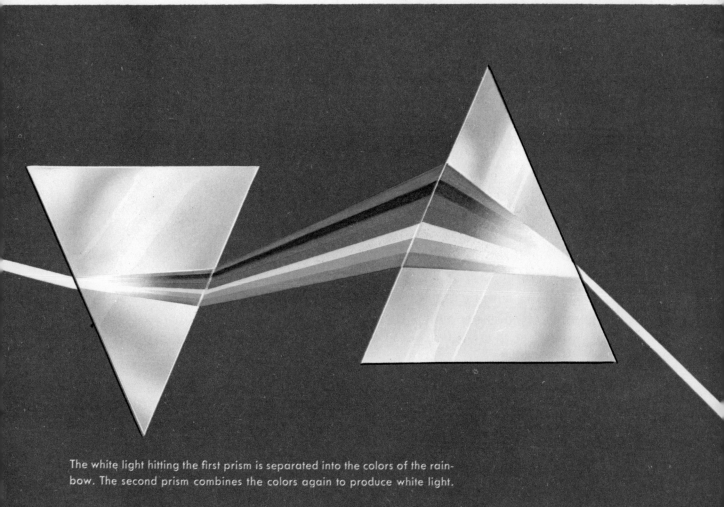

The white light hitting the first prism is separated into the colors of the rainbow. The second prism combines the colors again to produce white light.

When Newton first found that white light was composed

How are white light and color related? of different colors, he believed that the colors were produced by different types of light "corpuscles" or "bullets." One type of bullet produced red light, another blue light, another green light, and so forth. His light theory became known as the corpuscular theory of light.

At about the same time that Newton lived, a Dutch scientist, Christian Huygens, was also studying light. It was he who originated the idea that light is a series of waves (much the same as those created by throwing a stone into a pond of water), with every point on a wavefront of light being a new source of wavelets and thus creating an indefinite number of wavefronts.

For many years, scientists studying light and color were divided into two groups; one group favored Newton's theory of light and the other favored Huygen's theory of light. However, there were some scientists who were not fully satisfied with either theory since neither could be proven true under all conditions. Many modifications of both theories were suggested, but none of these modifications was acceptable since scientists sought a theory that applied at all times under all conditions.

At the beginning of this book, in describing what is light, we noted that light is a form of energy that radiates in all directions from its source. This idea that light is a form of energy was formulated by the German scientist,

Max Planck in 1900 in his now famous *Quantum Theory*. He said that radiant energy such as light is composed basically of tiny irreducible bits of energy called *quanta* which travel or radiate from the light source.

Five years after Planck announced his theory, Albert Einstein proposed a more exact definition of the energy that causes light. While studying the composition of the atom, Einstein came to the conclusion that light, in spite of its wave nature, must be composed of an energy particle of the atom which he called a *photon*.

Today, despite the recognition of the greatness of the inventors of these various theories, scientists still are unable to decide upon a single theory of light. They accept the idea that light is a form

ern its behavior under certain conditions, but it will be up to the scientists of tomorrow — maybe one of you — to come up with the answer to: "What is light?"

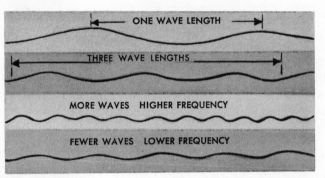

PARTS OF A WAVE

ONE WAVE LENGTH

THREE WAVE LENGTHS

MORE WAVES   HIGHER FREQUENCY

FEWER WAVES   LOWER FREQUENCY

What are the parts of a light wave?

To understand how a light wave travels and exactly what it is, it is best to study waves in water first, since you have all seen this kind of wave.

If you throw a pebble or stone into a pond or lake, it creates waves. The number of waves that comes to the shore varies, depending upon the size stone we throw into the lake. The number of waves, if measured for a specific period of time, say a minute, is known as *wave frequency*.

We can also study the length of the wave; that is, the distance from the crest (or top) of one wave to the crest of the next. This distance is known as *wave length*. Generally, the shorter the wave length the higher the frequency (greater the number of waves) and the longer the wave length the lower the frequency (fewer number of waves). Let's now apply this to the light waves.

of energy or radiation produced by the photon, but they also know that light travels like a wave. Thus, they accept the concept that light has two different disguises: first, when light travels from one place to another — from the sun to the earth or from an electric bulb to our eyes, or from an electric bulb to this page — the light travels as if it were a wave; secondly, when light is emitted by an object — such as light leaving the sun or leaving an electric bulb — or when light is absorbed by an object — such as a leaf taking in the light to produce its own food from carbon dioxide and water — the light acts as if it were a stream of "bullets" or photons.

Actually, no one today is certain exactly what light is. We know how it works and we have certain rules to gov-

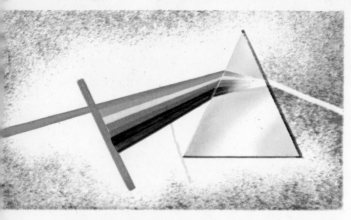

Color by absorption: The red glass plate absorbs practically all colors from the white light except the red, which passes through.

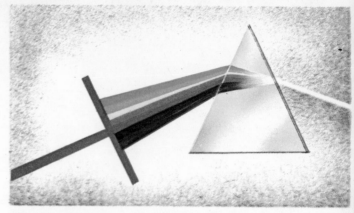

The blue glass plate absorbs practically all colors from the white light except the blue which passes through it unhampered.

How long are light waves?

Scientists have special instruments to measure the length and frequency of the different color light waves found in the white light spectrum. This measurement is exceedingly fine work since the wave length of light is very, very small. As a yardstick for measurement, the scientists have created a special measuring unit; they call this unit of wave length the *angstrom*. One angstrom is equal to four billionths of an inch, or in other words, in one inch there are 250,000,000 angstrom units.

Studying the spectrum, scientists found that the wave length of red light is considerably longer than the wave length of violet light. The red light wave is 7,600 angstroms in length or about $28/1,000,000$ (twenty-eight millionths) of an inch. The violet light wave is about half as long or 4,000 angstroms or $16/1,000,000$ (sixteen millionths) of an inch. The wave lengths of the other colors of the spectrum vary between these two extremes, getting shorter when going from red to orange to yellow to green to blue to indigo to violet.

Applying our knowledge of the relation of lengths and frequency in water waves, we can readily see that the longer wave lengths have lower frequencies than the shorter wave lengths. Thus, violet light has a higher frequency than any of the others, and red light has a lower frequency than any of the others.

Below, table of wave length of colors in the spectrum.

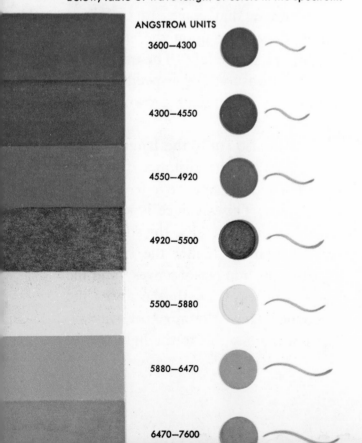

ANGSTROM UNITS

3600—4300

4300—4550

4550—4920

4920—5500

5500—5880

5880—6470

6470—7600

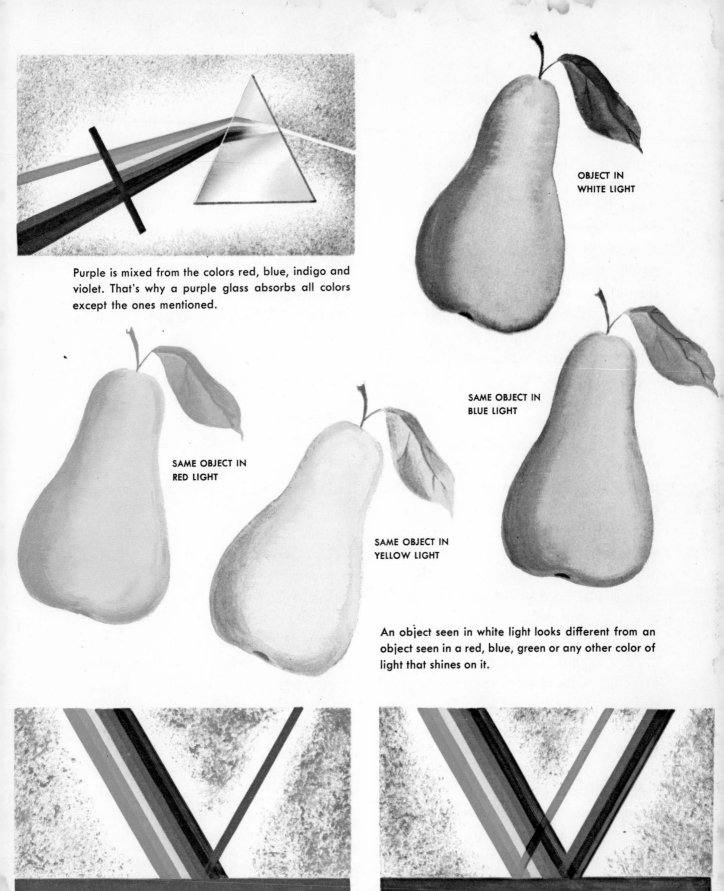

Purple is mixed from the colors red, blue, indigo and violet. That's why a purple glass absorbs all colors except the ones mentioned.

OBJECT IN
WHITE LIGHT

SAME OBJECT IN
RED LIGHT

SAME OBJECT IN
BLUE LIGHT

SAME OBJECT IN
YELLOW LIGHT

An object seen in white light looks different from an object seen in a red, blue, green or any other color of light that shines on it.

Colors by reflection: A blue surface will absorb practically all colors and reflect only blue.

The purple surface will absorb all colors and reflect only red, blue, indigo and violet.

37

If you look at a tree in the summertime during the day-time, its leaves look green. But if you look at the same tree at night, with only the stars above and with no other light, the leaves will look black (see illustrations, pages 36-37).

Why does an object have color?

Actually, the color of any object depends upon two things: (a) whether the object is opaque or transparent, and (b) the color of the light in which we are viewing the object. According to scientists, neither white nor black are really colors. White is the presence of all the colors of sunlight, while black is the lack of color.

An opaque object will reflect certain colors and will absorb the rest. The leaves on the tree we observed in the daylight in the summer appear green because the leaves reflect the green light waves of the sunlight and absorb the other colors. Those leaves at night appear black because there is no light that they can reflect. This lack of reflected colors is what produces black.

A transparent object transmits colors; that is, it permits the colors to pass through. Since it does not absorb certain colors and reflect others, it is clear and appears without any color, like ordinary window glass.

Translucent objects, on the other hand, diffuse the light waves that pass through them. We see the "color" of these objects on the basis of what type of light waves they permit to pass through and which they absorb. Thus, translucent objects can appear frosty or without color like plain glass, or they can have color.

Similarly, the color of the light in which we view an object will affect the color of that object. If we look at a ripe red apple in the sunlight, that apple will reflect the red light waves and absorb the others; thus, we say the apple is red. But if we looked at the same apple under a blue lamp bulb, the apple would appear to be black since there are no red light waves to be reflected by the apple.

Many of the colors we see around us are produced by paints or dyes. A tie is red because a special dye has been used to reflect the red light waves either from the sun or the standard white household electric bulb.

Can objects reflect more than one color?

However, these dyes and paints do not produce pure natural colors as found in the white light or sunlight spectrum. A yellow painted wall in white light will reflect some green or some yellow light waves. If most of the reflected light waves are yellow, we see a yellow wall. If there are a large number of green light waves mixed in with the yellow light waves, we see a yellow-green wall.

Similarly, if you have ever mixed water colors or paints, you have found that if you combine equal portions of blue and yellow pigment, you will make a green color. What happens when sunlight strikes the green paint on the wall? The blue paint will absorb the yellow

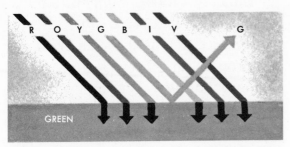

Green watercolors, consisting of mixed blue and yellow, reflect only green lightwaves, as the blue rays are absorbed by the yellow paint and the yellow by the blue paint parts.

light waves and the yellow paint will absorb the blue light waves (in addition to other colors), but since neither absorbs the green light waves, they will be reflected and you will see the green wall.

Why is the sky blue? At one time it was believed that the air was a blue gas and that was why the sky looked blue. Many other theories were advanced for the color of the sky, none of which was acceptable. Scientists sought an answer and they found it by studying smoke coming out of a chimney.

If you watch fine smoke rising into the air on a cloudy day, you will find that the smoke looks blue as it passes in front of a dark background. Make sure you are watching fine thin smoke against a darkened sky or you may not be able to see the blue.

This was the scientists' clue. The light reaching the smoke, which consists of many tiny particles of carbon, dust, unburnt fragments and other materials, was partially broken up by those particles. The blue light waves, which are exceedingly short, are bounced off by the particles, whereas the other colored light rays continue unaffected. The bouncing off, both as reflection and re-

In the light of the flashlight, water with milk in it will appear blue.

fraction, of the short blue light waves makes the smoke look blue.

The air about the earth is composed of many tiny particles, including dust and water vapor. As the sunlight passes through the air, the shorter blue light waves are reflected and refracted by the particles while the other colored light waves, being longer, are unaffected and are not reflected by the water vapor or dust in the air.

The blue waves spread all over the sky so that it appears blue. Here is a simple project to let you prove that fine particles will bend the blue light waves.

All you need for this project is a transparent water glass, water, a few drops of milk and a flashlight.

Pour a few drops of milk into a transparent glass filled with water. If you want to be exact and have an eye dropper, drop about 10 to 15 drops of the milk into the water. This milky-water is similar to the air above the earth that contains water vapor and dust.

Pull down the shades or put out the light in the room so that it is dark. Now, set your flashlight about one to two inches from the glass so that it is at right angles to the side of the glass. Turn the flashlight on. The water looks blue! The milk in the water has bent the blue light rays which are in the white beam of light from the flashlight, just as the moisture and dust bend the blue light rays coming from the sun.

HOW TO MAKE A COLOR WHEEL

From our study of color we know that white is the presence of all the colors of the spectrum. Here is a simple color wheel to help you prove this scientific observation.

Cut a circle of cardboard about 3 to 4 inches in diameter and divide it into six parts as shown in the diagram. Use water colors, paints or crayons to fill in the colors as indicated.

Set a small nail through the center, gluing it in place. When it is thoroughly dried, set the nail into a hand-drill as shown so that the disc can turn freely. Holding the drill so that you can watch the disc, turn the drill quickly until all the colors blend. Because there are many different types of drills, it is impossible to tell you exactly how fast to turn it. You will have to experiment. When you reach the right speed, all the colors will blend together and it will appear as if a white disc is at the end of the drill. Make certain that the drill you use can reach a very high speed when you are turning.

Light project #14

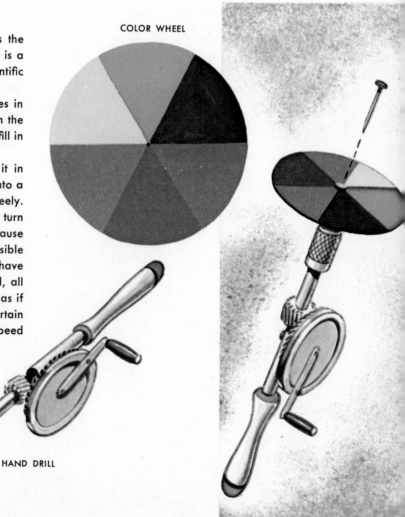

COLOR WHEEL

HAND DRILL

Polarized Light

One of the properties of light, according to scientists, is its traveling in wave form as it goes from one place to another. The light from a source travels as a series of crests and troughs much like a wave in water. We can create such waves with a piece of string or rope. If you tie one end of the string to a door knob and hold the other end in one hand, you will be able to produce a wave by moving your wrist up and down. This type of wave, moving up and down, is known as a *vertical transverse wave* because it vibrates in a vertical plane, an imaginary vertical surface. On the other hand, if you move your wrist from side to side, you will produce another type of a wave; it is known as a *horizontal transverse wave,* vibrating in a horizontal plane. Now, still holding the rope,

What are polarized light waves?

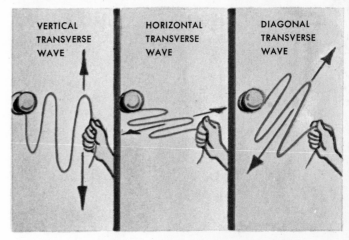

Like the waves in a string made by moving your wrist in all directions, light waves flow in different planes.

you can move your wrist along a diagonal — to the right as you go up and to the left as you go down. You have now produced another type of a wave different from either the vertical or horizontal transverse wave.

We know that light travels as a wave from place to place. But what kind of a wave is it? Actually, the light wave scientists talk about is a combination of several types of waves. It travels as a horizontal transverse wave, a vertical transverse wave and many types of diagonal transverse waves. In effect, it is a combination of waves each flowing in a different plane. If we isolate or separate any of these waves, that is, single out one wave in a given plane, we have polarized the light wave.

We have learned that light is transmitted by waves that travel horizontally, vertically and transversely. When a light ray passes through a polarized lens, part of the waves are blocked out, reducing the quantity of light. If we now pass what was left through a second polarized lens which is turned at 90° to the first one, no light at all will pass. In the illustration on page 41, you can create waves in the string. These waves move freely in all directions. In the illustration on this page, the slit in the box allows only vertical waves. If you turn the box 90°, only the horizontal motion is possible. If you combined two boxes, one with a horizontal slit and one with a vertical slit, you would find that no wave motion at all would reach the doorknob.

string through a vertical slit, as between the slats of a chair back or a specially cut cardboard box (see illustration). If you move your wrist up and down, the transverse wave produced will pass through the slit in the chair back and reach the door knob. However, what if you moved your wrist from side to side? You will create a horizontal transverse wave, but that wave will stop when it reaches the slit in the chair. You have just polarized the horizontal wave; you have stopped it from passing through the chair back while the vertical wave could pass through.

Similarly, we can do the same thing with light waves by using special materials or lenses. These materials consist of millions of small crystals shaped like needles and they permit only those light waves which vibrate in their direction to pass through the material. The material used is known as a *polarized plate* or *lens*.

Normally, polarized plates or lenses are used in pairs. When the two special lenses are placed so that their "slits" are

Let us return to the string for a moment to demonstrate an-

How can a wave be polarized?

other effect that would make it easier to understand light wave polarization. Suppose you leave the string tied to the door knob, but you now pass the

parallel, they let through only those waves that are in the same plane. When the slits are crossed or placed at right angles, they permit no light to pass through.

Actually, light is being polarized all

Why do we polarize light waves?

around us every day. It is polarized when sunlight is reflected and refracted by moisture and dust in the air and when light is reflected from very smooth non-metallic surfaces which act as mirrors. However, our eyes cannot tell the difference between polarized and non-polarized light waves. Yet, when we take photographs and want to eliminate unwanted reflections, such as the reflection from the glass in a picture frame, we use polarizing lenses to do this job. Similarly, when we are observing an object under a microscope, we can eliminate the unwanted reflections which may occur. Again, we use polarizing lenses to do the job. Similarly, polarized glass used in windshields of automobiles and motorboats reduces the glare from the sun and from the headlights of approaching vehicles.

The Speed of Light

It was not until man began to explore

Why did scientists measure the speed of light?

the universe with telescopes that he began to consider the question of the speed of light.

The renewed interest in science late in the sixteenth century resulted in men beginning to look for the answers to how and why. Scientists started to discover the speed of light because they were curious. They knew that you saw lightning before you heard thunder. They knew that sound traveled slower than light. But they wanted to know how fast did sound travel, how fast did light travel. The seeking of the answers to these and many other questions has always been the sign of a scientist.

In the early seventeenth century, the

How was the speed of light first measured?

famous Italian scientist, Galileo, tried to measure the speed of light as it traveled from a lantern on a hilltop a mile away from where he stood. The inadequacy of his timing instruments made it impossible for him to measure the speed of light accurately over so short a distance. Today, with our knowledge of the speed of light, we know that Galileo would have required a timing instrument that could measure less than one hundred thousandth of a second — that is the time light needs to travel one mile.

About fifty years after Galileo's experiment, the Danish astronomer, Ole Römer, in 1676, measured the speed of

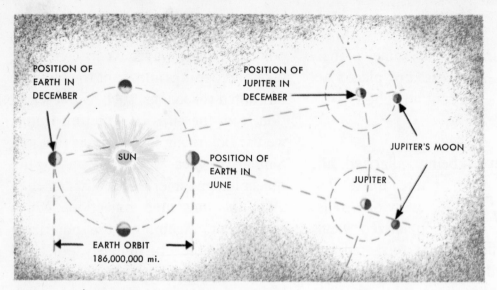

POSITION OF
EARTH IN
DECEMBER

POSITION OF
JUPITER IN
DECEMBER

JUPITER'S MOON

SUN

POSITION OF
EARTH IN
JUNE

JUPITER

EARTH ORBIT
186,000,000 mi.

The Danish astronomer Ole Römer measured the speed of light by observing the eclipses of one of the twelve moons of the planet Jupiter.

light by observing one of the eleven moons of the planet Jupiter. He assumed that light, like sound, traveled at a specific speed. It was known that the moons of Jupiter travel at a set speed around the planet and that it would take one of the moons 42½ hours to revolve around Jupiter, or in other words, that every 42½ hours it would be eclipsed by (disappear behind) the planet. He could make a time schedule of the eclipses for the entire year. But he had made his first observation in June, when Jupiter is nearest to the earth, and he found out in December, when Jupiter is farthest from the earth, that his schedule was off by 1000 seconds. (His schedule was 1000 seconds behind in December.) Römer knew that the distance across the orbit of the earth was 186,000,000 miles. He explained his schedule being off 1000 seconds by concluding that it took the light 1000 seconds to travel 186,000,000 miles, or 186,000 miles in one second. At that speed, if light could bend around the earth, it would circle the earth 7½ times in one second.

As scientists learned more about the universe and developed more precise measuring instruments, they made many attempts to measure the speed of light more precisely. One of the most famous of these experiments was conducted by the American scientist, Albert A. Michelson, in 1902. He used a precision machine and measured the speed of light as it traveled to and bounced back from a mirror that was 22 miles away.

What is the speed of light?

The light traveled that distance in less than a thousandth of a second. He was able to make the measurements because his distance was greater and his instruments more precise than those which Galileo used almost 300 years before him. Michelson determined the speed of light at 186,284 miles per second.

It is interesting to note that the Michelson speed was less than one percent different from that of Römer,

The light waves are only a small part of the electromagnetic spectrum.

which was calculated with much poorer instruments some 225 years earlier. Scientists have conducted many additional experiments to measure the speed of light using different methods. On the average, these have shown that light travels at 186,282 miles per second.

We use the speed of light as a measuring stick in studying the universe. Some of the distances from earth are small enough that we can talk about them in miles. For example, the moon is about 240,000 miles away from the earth; the sun is about 93,000,000 miles away from the earth.

How long is a "light year?"

However, when we begin to measure distances to the stars, we find that we have to work with very large numbers. Just as scientists developed a special unit of measurement for the wave lengths of the different colors, so have scientists developed a special unit for measuring distance in space. It is a *light year*.

A light year is the distance that light travels in a single year. This is a large number considering that light travels about 186,000 miles per second. A light year is roughly 6,000,000,000,000 (six trillion) miles. Alpha Centauri, the nearest brilliant star, is more than 4 light years away.

Rays Other Than Light

Again we must return to the basic question: what is light? As you recall, scientists now believe that light is a form of energy that radiates waves in all directions. Let us pause for a moment to consider one essential word, "radiates."

What is the "electromagnetic spectrum?"

Have you ever walked into the sunlight after being in the cool shade? Even if you had your eyes closed so that you

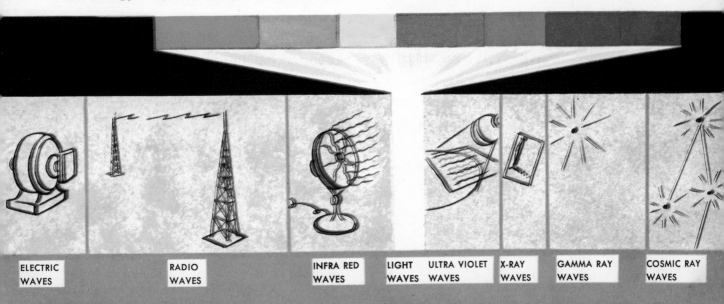

| ELECTRIC WAVES | RADIO WAVES | INFRA RED WAVES | LIGHT WAVES | ULTRA VIOLET WAVES | X-RAY WAVES | GAMMA RAY WAVES | COSMIC RAY WAVES |

could not see the sun, you would still know you were in the sunlight. Why? You would "feel" the sun since it would warm your body. But instead of walking into the sunlight, suppose you walked near a burning fire. Again you would "feel" the fire even if you did not see it. The fire, like the sun, is "radiating" heat, which is a form of energy.

Actually, we are continually surrounded by radiations. The sun is constantly bombarding the earth with cosmic rays, a form of radiation. The fire in the stove, the electric iron with which we iron clothes, the incandescent electric bulb by which we read — all are emitting heat, a form of radiation. Radio and radar, which we use to send and receive messages during the day or night, in clear weather or in fog, use a special type of radiation. Even the electricity we use in our homes is a form of radiation.

Scientists have put all the many types of radiations into a single category which they have labelled the *electromagnetic spectrum.*

The electromagnetic spectrum consists of waves whose wave lengths — the distance from the crest of one wave to the crest of the next — are over 20 miles long to wave lengths smaller than a billionth of an inch. We find that the very long waves are those radiated by electricity and radio transmitters, while the very short ones, the cosmic rays, are those radiated by the sun. Those with longer wave lengths have a lower frequency than those with shorter wave lengths.

What is the "visible spectrum?" That portion of the electromagnetic spectrum (or all forms of radiation) that we are able to see, is known as the *visible spectrum.* Light waves as a form of radiation are the only part of the electromagnetic spectrum that we can see with our eyes.

The visible spectrum extends from the red wave lengths, which are the longest of the visible spectrum, to the violet wave lengths, which are the shortest of the visible spectrum.

What are light's neighbors in the electromagnetic spectrum? Heat rays, the warmth we receive from the sun or from a fire, are part of the electromagnetic spectrum. These rays were identified by the famous English scientist, Sir William Herschel, about 1800. He found that these waves had longer wave lengths than red light; these waves are known as infra-red rays or waves. The prefix *infra* means below in Latin; infra-red rays are below red light waves in the electromagnetic spectrum—they have longer wave lengths and lower frequencies.

Shortly after Sir William Herschel reported his finding of infra-red rays, a German chemist, Johann Wilhelm Ritter, discovered special waves or rays at the other end of the visible light spectrum. These are known as *ultra-violet rays* or waves. The prefix *ultra* means beyond in Latin; ultra-violet rays are beyond the violet light waves — they have shorter wave lengths and higher frequencies than violet light waves.

As we increase the temperature of an object, it will radiate heat. If we increase the temperature high enough, the object will not only radiate heat but it will also radiate light waves.

How can we take photographs without light?

We use this scientific information in our everyday life since this is how the ordinary household electric light bulb works. There is a very fine wire inside the glass shell and we increase its temperature by sending electricity (also a form of radiation) through the wire. The wire becomes very hot and radiates heat and light. The same is true if we placed a piece of iron in a very hot fire. First, the iron would become too hot to touch. If we provided enough heat (and this varies depending upon the object we use), it will eventually glow with a red light.

We use infra-red rays in many ways. In industrial plants, for example, special infra-red bulbs dry paint on automobiles quickly. We also have photographic film that is sensitive only to infra-red waves. This film is very useful in photographing on cloudy, misty days since the infra-red and red waves pass through the haze and mist more easily than the other visible waves. It is possible, by using this special film, to take a picture in complete darkness using two hot objects that emit infra-red waves that will be reflected by the subject which is being photographed.

There are waves other than light waves that will pass not only through our bodies but even through heavy steel.

What are X-Rays?

These waves are thousands of times shorter than the shortest visible light rays and have much higher frequencies, somewhere near a billion billion waves per second.

These special waves were discovered by a German scientist, Wilhelm Roentgen, in 1895. In studying the waves emitted by a cathode ray tube, he found waves that would darken photographic film just as visible light waves do. He also discovered that these waves would make materials fluoresce just as ultraviolet waves do. He called them *X-rays* because in mathematics, *x* stands for an unknown quantity.

Today these rays or waves are known as X-rays or Roentgen rays. The X-ray spectrum consists of a group of waves of varying wave lengths. The longer of these, known as "soft X-rays," can penetrate only soft substances, such as flesh, and are used to photograph bones or organs in the body. The shorter wave length X-rays, known as "hard rays," can penetrate thick, dense substances, such as iron or steel, and are used in industry to examine large metal machine parts for possible hidden cracks.

Light rays — radiation — observed since man is on earth, has still not yielded all its secrets. With the beginning of the space age and the research of cosmic and atomic radiation, we might be able to get closer to the answer of: What is light?

A New Kind of Light: Laser Light

The laser is a new kind of light. It has been made by man and cannot be found anywhere in nature. The device that makes this kind of light is also called a laser.

Light from a candle, the sun, or an electric light bulb speeds away from the source of the light in all different directions. These sources of light are made up of several different frequencies, or wavelengths. Laser light, on the other hand, is so pure in color that it can be made up of a single frequency, or wavelength. All the waves of laser light travel in the same direction.

There are two main kinds of lasers, solid and gas. A solid laser uses a substance like ruby which can be caused to give out or emit a beam of laser light. The beam is intensely bright and lasts only a fraction of a millionth of a second. Because it is so intense, it is very hot. Beams from ruby lasers have been used to weld loose retinas in human eyes. The flash of laser light, though hot, lasts so short a time that it does not burn the tissues surrounding the retina.

A second kind of laser, the gas laser, produces a continuous beam of light. It can be used to vaporize metal so that scientists can make a quick analysis of the metal. It can punch holes in substances that are hard to melt.

Because all the waves of a laser beam travel in the same direction, the laser beam is very narrow. It does not spread out like the beam of light from a flashlight. The moon is 238,856 miles away from the earth. If we aimed a laser beam at the moon, upon striking the moon's surface, the beam would illuminate an area only one mile in diameter. If we could build a searchlight powerful enough to reach the moon and illuminate it, its rays would spread out so much that they would cover an area six times the diameter of the moon, or a circle 12,960 miles wide.

The narrowness of the laser beam means that we can focus a great deal of energy in a small area. We could use a laser beam to boil coffee in a pot 1,000 miles from the laser!

Because of the very pure frequency of a laser beam, it can be used to carry broadcast messages, as radio and television waves are used. In 1965 all of New York's seven television channels broadcast on one laser beam. Scientists are working on ways to send thousands of messages at one time on one laser beam. Not only can a laser beam carry all these messages, but it carries them free of static.

The laser was invented in 1958 by Professor Charles Townes, of Columbia University, and Dr. Arthur Schawlow, of the Bell Telephone Laboratories. In 1960 Professor Theodore Maiman made the first working laser. A year later Dr. Ali Javan made the first gas (or continuous) laser.